The ART *and*
PRACTICE
of
LOVING

The ART and PRACTICE of LOVING

Frank Andrews, Ph.D.

JEREMY P. TARCHER, INC.
Los Angeles

Library of Congress Cataloging-in-Publication Data

Copyright © 1991 by Frank Andrews

Library of Congress Cataloging-in-Publication Data

Andrews, Frank, Ph. D.
    The art and practice of loving / Frank Andrews.—1st ed.
        p.   cm.
    ISBN 0-87477-606-6
    1. Love.   I. Title.
BF575.L8A53   1990   90-19847
152.4'1—dc20   CIP

Jeremy P. Tarcher, Inc.
5858 Wilshire Blvd., Suite 200
Los Angeles, CA 90036

Distributed by St. Martin's Press, New York

Design by Deborah Daly

Manufactured in the United States of America
10   9   8   7   6   5   4   3   2   1

First Edition

To Karen and Elizabeth—
May theirs be a generation of peace and love.

CONTENTS

ACKNOWLEDGMENTS

I am deeply indebted to each of my many teachers, and to the hundreds of students and friends who have opened their hearts to me that I might learn. In particular I thank Hal Zina Bennett, Peter Beren, and Larry Forsberg for encouraging the book at crucial times and contributing their own indispensable expertise. I thank H. Michael Ellerby for supporting both me and the project from the very beginning, and for pushing for the highest possible standards of content and expression. I thank Connie Zweig for her work as editor, Paul Murphy for overseeing design and production, and Jeremy Tarcher for his vision of the project, which has made all the difference to the book and to my growth.

I thank Karen, Elizabeth, and Jeanie for inspiration and never-failing support, and Elizabeth for invaluable creative editing.

When I think of my own path of loving, my tongue knots up at putting into words the gratitude I feel. I have followed a trail blazed eons ago and built by countless people with their laughter, their tears, and their loving. To them, my deepest gratitude. And to the Power that put them here, there are no appropriate words, except to recommit my life to following a path of loving.

The day will come when,
after harnessing space,
  the winds,
    the tides,
      and gravitation,
we shall harness for God the energies of love.
And on that day, for the second time
In the history of the world,
  we shall have discovered fire.

TEILHARD DE CHARDIN

PREFACE

Earth's the right place for love:
I don't know where it's likely to go better.

ROBERT FROST

This is a guidebook for loving, deeply and continually, regardless of what happens to you as you go through life. You may be young or old, single, happily or unhappily married, widowed, or divorced. You may be bored with routine or moving to something completely new, pregnant for the first time or watching your last child leave home, starting a new job or losing or retiring from your old one, moving into your first home or into a nursing home, surrounded by friends and relatives or all alone, fit and healthy or living with a terminal illness. Whatever your activities or circumstances, life challenges you to appreciate and celebrate them, regardless of how much you may like or dislike them, to breathe care and joy into whatever you do.

Oh, the worst of all tragedies is not to die young but to live until I am seventy-five and yet not ever truly to have lived.

MARTIN LUTHER KING, JR.

Millions long for immortality who don't know what to do with themselves on a rainy Sunday afternoon.

SUSAN ERTZ

Despite all the attention our society pays to achieving success by reaching goals, it's obvious that success is not a state people reach—success is an internal experience. Just succeeding in reaching a goal will not by itself bring the delight and satisfaction it seemed to promise.

I

Although we all see people successfully reach their goals in education and work, we also see them lose interest and meaning in their careers, and sometimes they even burn out. We see people marry the *perfect* person and raise the *perfect* children of their dreams, yet they are unable to sustain real affection, warmth, and intimacy within their families. We see people successfully build up their bank accounts yet never experience the wealth and security they thought money would provide. Even those most skilled at reaching goals may lack the skills of creating enthusiasm and delight out of the favorable circumstances in their lives. They can get the job done, but cannot use either the process or the results to produce the deeper satisfaction and joy they dreamed about.

So faith, hope, love abide, these three; but the greatest of these is love. Make love your aim.

ST. PAUL

A new commandment I give to you, that you love one another.

JESUS

Let the disciple cultivate love without measure toward all beings. Let him cultivate toward the whole world, above, below, around, a heart of love unstinted. . . . For in all the world this state of heart is best.

BUDDHA

Countless wise men and women have taught that the major purpose of life is to learn and practice not the art of reaching goals, but the art of loving. These experts, whose recorded teachings date back five thousand years or more, made loving their ultimate concern, and used the path of loving as a spiritual path, a path to God. Regardless of any relationship you may have with an established religion, loving whatever comes to you in life is a spiritual discipline.

This way of life, though filled with familiar people, activities, and objects, never stops taking on new beauty and meaning as you gain expertise at following it. No matter how far you have come on a path of loving, you can never imagine what life will be like around the next bend.

> *Who is the man who walks the Way?*
>   *Opening the window, he steals the moonlight;*
>   *Moving his seat, he faces the clear-flowing stream.*
>
>   RAKAN

You spend a great portion of your life working at *minor* activities rather than *major* ones—for example, washing the dishes, talking to a friend, or driving to work. Therefore, it is precisely in these daily activities that you walk your loving path, or else you have at most a few isolated loving events. Regardless of how you fare with major activities, you need the skills to love even the smallest creature and the humblest activity in order to cherish the day-to-day circumstances of life. You don't have to gain evidence of success or find somebody mind-shatteringly wonderful in order to be able to live in love.

A journey of a thousand miles must begin with a single step.

                                      LAO TZU

Even if you are on a long trip, it is still the little steps that get you there. That is good for those of us wanting to practice loving, because there are so many little steps to practice on—like taking a shower, fixing supper, and listening to children laugh.

> *Every prophet and every saint hath a way,*
>   *but it leads to God:*
> *All the ways are really one.*
>
>   RUMI

This path with its joys and challenges is well trodden; it is worn by the caring, laughter, and tears of thousands of generations of our ancestors who have opened their hearts to their world, their fellows, their work, and their lives. Religious and spiritual journeyers from all traditions—counselors, healers, poets, writers, philosophers, social scientists, and self-reflective natural lovers—have discovered that a particular set of habits in the form of thoughts, attitudes, approaches, beliefs, and practices made them better at loving. This book can teach you those habits.

Ask yourself, and yourself alone, one question—Does this path have a heart? All paths are the same; they lead nowhere. They are paths going through the bush or into the bush. . . . Does this path have a heart? If it does, the path is good; if it doesn't, it is of no use.

DON JUAN (CARLOS CASTANEDA)

Where do you look to answer Don Juan's question: Does this path have a heart? Certainly not to your circumstances —job, family, accomplishments, or home. You have to look into your own experience on the path to see how much heart you have put into it. However you answer, the truth is that you can always put more heart into your path. We are never fully accomplished at turning living into loving.

Take your shoes off of your feet, for the place on which you are standing is holy ground.

GOD, TO MOSES, FROM THE BURNING BUSH

> *Earth's crammed with heaven,*
> *And every common bush afire with God;*
> *But only he who sees takes off his shoes;*
> *The rest sit round it and pluck blackberries.*

ELIZABETH BARRETT BROWNING

You can learn to see the fire of God in every common bush—not by hunting around until you find an especially spectacular bush, but by cultivating your own loving approach to all the bushes in your world.

> *The world will change because of your smile. . . .*
> *To sit, to smile, to look at things and really see them—*
> *These form the basis of peace work.*
>
> THICH NHAT HANH

There are more than merely personal reasons for you to commit to a path of loving. Humanity has developed such enormous capacity for both nurturing and destroying that loving is demanded of us as a service to all of life, both present and future. The major organ of society is the human heart, yet never has the world known such a need for *heart* wisdom, a wisdom based on loving.

If we are to live at all, we must live together in peace and dignity, and we will live together in peace and dignity only by loving. Furthermore, as the earth is being pushed rapidly to the limits of its carrying capacity, it will continue to sustain life only if it is treated with the respect born of love. The greatest offering we can make, to the world and to posterity, is to love.

After all, we live on a beautiful planet, and we share it with such diverse and fascinating fellow creatures. We have a rich cultural heritage from those who have gone before us, people who have poured out their strength to survive and to secure the lives of those who followed after them. Their vision was that their children would live in joy and peace. We are their children. Only by living in joy and peace, only by going beyond our never-ending desires and fears and turning life on earth into a continual celebration of the lovable world in which we live will we crown with triumph the lives of those who have lived and loved before us.

How to Use This Book

You can get something from a book. That something may be so important as to lead you to the recognition of the real thing.

IDRIES SHAH

Read for the sake of practicing, not for reading's sake.

SAI BABA

This book consists of three parts: practices, quotes, and text. The practices are mostly pleasant ones, designed to strengthen your ability to create loving experiences and remove blocks that keep you from loving. Though sometimes deceivingly simple, some of them, in identical or related form, have served as lifelong spiritual practices for countless people before you. The practice of loving builds upon itself, so that as you progress, your rate of reward will increase. This means that the work requires patience and trust—trust that the best ideas and practices that humanity has developed for fostering loving are in fact valuable and will work for you.

The quotations, mainly from religious or spiritual traditions, are intended to stand for all those who have passed this way before.

Ask, and it will be given you; seek, and you will find; knock, and it will be opened to you. For every one who asks receives, and he who seeks finds, and to him who knocks it will be opened.

JESUS

Hasten slowly and ye shall soon arrive.

MILAREPA

When I read a book, I like to relax, put my feet up, and underline a few ideas I especially like. If the book has practices, I enjoy thinking of friends who would be helped by doing them. While that relaxed approach is fun, it does not help me develop my skills. Just as you learn any set of skills, gaining expertise at opening and warming your heart takes knowledge, commitment, practice, and coaching.

You have proved many times that you have the ability to love. You can cultivate that ability with this workbook, which addresses both your mind and your heart. It takes work and practice to build new habits and strengthen the skills with which you can turn living into loving. Inspiring anecdotes might motivate you, but they will not do the job. Only you can do the job, by practicing, alone and maybe with others.

Do not do the practices once and leave it at that. Your response to any one of them will change from one day, month, or year to the next. No matter how many times you do a practice, it will remain an invitation to return to it so you can learn more about yourself and loving, deepen your commitment to loving, and push through your barriers to loving.

The aim of all spiritual practice is love.
SAI BABA

Love is a product of habit.
LUCRETIUS

Many of these practices involve writing in a journal that you keep for that purpose. While there is nothing wrong with merely reading and thinking about what you read, writing can be more powerful. Through writing you reflect on your experiences in the practices and explore more deeply, more carefully, how various ideas relate to your own life. Because you record these explorations, you can later reread them and pick up where you left off. A written practice seems finite, do-able, rather than overwhelming. Of course, talking over your explorations with other people is valuable too, but appropriate people are often hard to find. A journal can be carried wherever you go, inviting you into its pages whenever you have a moment. It never condemns you, and it keeps your confidences. Your journal will be your best friend on your path of loving.

The result of a practice is never *right* or *wrong*, no result is any *better* or *worse* than another. All practices and their results are part of your lifelong loving path. If the intention of a practice is to love something and instead you draw a blank or feel pain or sadness, that experience is useful. An athlete sometimes feels pain, rather than strength, from a particular exercise, but that does not mean she should have skipped the exercise. You will learn and grow from each practice, regardless of its particular results. The payoff is not in any one practice, but in your overall life.

While you can read this book for ideas or inspiration, it is also a workbook for a lifetime. Our culture offers few tools for opening and warming the heart. Instead, it teaches us powerful tools of the mind to analyze and control the outside world. We work so hard to learn those tools and master that world. Here are a few tools for delighting in the process, for loving on the way. Surely they deserve some work too.

When you choose to take a path of loving, you are at once embracing your humanity and trusting the world. It is the most loving act of which you are capable.

> *We shall not cease from exploration*
> *And the end of all our exploring*
> *Will be to arrive where we started*
> *And know the place for the first time.*
>
> T. S. ELIOT

> *Arise from sleep, old cat,*
> *   And with great yawns and stretchings—*
> *Amble out for love.*
>
> ISSA

1 ❦ LOVING—A HEARTFELT YES!

If I speak in the tongues of men and of angels, but have not love, I am a noisy gong or a clanging cymbal. And if I have prophetic powers, and understand all mysteries and all knowledge, and if I have all faith, so as to remove mountains, but have not love, I am nothing. If I give away all I have, and if I deliver my body to be burned, but have not love, I gain nothing.

ST. PAUL

Where love is, what can be wanting?
Where it is not, what can possibly be profitable?
ST. AUGUSTINE

*I*magine living the same life you do now, only loving deeply and continually—delighting in the warmth of your morning shower, relishing the smell of breakfast cooking, celebrating with the birds on your way to work, enjoying driving the roadways, feeling bonds of cooperation with your co-workers, cherishing your family members, and deeply appreciating whatever and whoever is at hand. Visualize going through the activities of a typical day while deeply caring about what you are doing, a day in which sensitivity, affection, warmth, and wonder fill the moments. That love-filled life is your birthright as a human being.

You probably share society's deep conviction that you love as a reaction to what happens to you when you encounter an object especially worthy of love—that your loving is an automatic reaction to someone or something especially lovable. If so, statements like those that head this chapter, though they may be good advice, seem impossible to act upon.

However, the great truth is that you can learn to love, deeply and continually, regardless of circumstances, in much the same way you can learn to perform a sport or play a musical instrument. Society focuses on finding especially lovable objects, but you are likely to keep the same family, work, and home for much of your life, so you are not likely to find more love by finding more lovable objects. The focus belongs on you—the one doing the loving. It is your skill and your will that can turn living into loving. The ideas and practices in this book are dedicated to your gaining that skill and will.

What Does Loving Mean to You?

> *How do I love thee? Let me count the ways.*
> ELIZABETH BARRETT BROWNING

A useful first step in making progress in any area is uncovering what you already know about it, the meanings you bring to it. People cling to what they already know about a subject and resist accepting anything different, even if only to try out a new idea to see how it works. Through your life experiences and the teachings of your culture, you have no doubt formulated many meanings of loving. Some of what you know helps you in loving more deeply, and some of it gets in the way. So it is worthwhile to examine what you currently associate with loving.

❦ ———————————————————————— ❦

Practice 1

WHAT DOES LOVING MEAN TO YOU?

Head a page in your journal What Does Loving Mean to Me? Then list meanings that come to mind when you ask yourself that question. Spend at least a few minutes writing just one or two key words that allow you to recall each meaning easily. Go for quantity of meanings, even if some of them contradict each other. When you think you have listed them all, close your eyes and ask yourself, "What else does loving mean to me?"

When you have exhausted your list for the moment, look over the items to see which ones might contribute to your becoming more loving; for example, "Loving means I am fulfilling the purpose for which I was placed on this earth." Also, consider which ones might get in the way; for example, "Loving someone means having to give in to that person." "Loving someone is a way to get hurt." "I'm too old (unattractive, shy, thin) to love someone."

As you proceed through this book, your beliefs about the meanings of loving will change with your experiences. Return to this practice from time to time, and your answers will reflect your progress.

Practice 2

RECALL TIMES YOU HAVE TRULY LOVED

In this practice you recall and re-vision occasions throughout your life when you have loved with special intensity. This will sharpen your vision of a more loving life and get you in the habit of putting your attention on loving. Before long you may be able to do this practice at any time and recall as much intense loving within the preceding day or hour as you now can recall from a lifetime.

Head a page in your journal Times I Have Truly Loved. Then think through your entire life and list the times that stand out in your memory. Again, go for quantity, listing whatever comes to mind. Amplify each item on your list by noting specific places, people, animals, thoughts, feelings, and actions.

Close your eyes and relive in your imagination especially loving occasions. These memories of loving are treasures you can experience whenever you choose. Use them any time you want to move into a more loving frame of mind or to appreciate further the richest times in your life. Do not be afraid of overusing a particular memory—from some of them you can derive lifelong delight.

 ———————————————————————————

Loving Is Living a Heartfelt Yes

Love is the affirmative of affirmatives.

RALPH WALDO EMERSON

When it is "Yes," a young Naga girl in an instant attains Buddhahood.
When it is "No," the most learned Zensho while alive falls into hell.

YOKA DAISHI

As you reflect upon times you have loved, you will note first of all that loving is not just a thought, feeling, or action, but all three—loving is an experience. Loving experiences are sometimes so strong that they overwhelm you, and sometimes they are just a wink or a touch in the middle of a busy day. In order to distinguish among them, here is a list of thirty labels for what I call the *heartwarmings* of love.

affection	connectedness	peace
alertness	curiosity	regard
appreciation	delight	respect
attention	enjoyment	responsiveness
awareness	enthusiasm	sensitivity
awe	interest	surrender
caring	intimacy	tenderness
celebration	joy	thankfulness
cherishing	liking	warmth
concern	oneness	wonder

These heartwarming experiences are what this book is about; I sum them up with the word *love*.

What all these experiences have in common is a positive response to whatever is being loved. Loving is living a heartfelt *yes*, a yes that warms your heart. A loving experience is one in which you approach the object with a positive attitude, think positively about it, and act openly toward it. You can mix love into any experience by mixing some yes into how you interpret it.

If you notice that you are bored with whatever is at hand, you can engage yourself in it with a heartfelt yes, and your experience changes first to interest and then to enthusiasm. If you notice that you are alienated from someone, you can warm up to him by interpreting him with a heartfelt yes, and your experience changes to appreciation, caring, or even to cherishing. The path of loving is the path of yes.

Appreciate each heartwarming experience when you have it. When you are before a tree, love the tree. When you are before a leaf, love the leaf. You need not rank one experience as greater than the other, even though you rake up the leaf and put it in the compost. Defining some heartwarmings to be less than loving leads to experiencing them as less than loving. Because they are therefore less rewarding to you, your narrow definition of loving will cause you to love less often.

 ———————————————————

Practice 3

RELIVING THE HEARTWARMINGS OF LOVE

Each of the heartwarmings listed above catches a slightly different nuance of the experience of loving. In this practice, you relive times in your past when you had these experiences. This will broaden your appreciation of the scope of loving and will also lead you to acknowledge that you are, and always have been, a lover (one who loves). You will also be rehearsing the future, since you repeat in reality the patterns you rehearse in imagination.

Take one of the meanings of love from the list—for

example, *wonder*. Head a page in your journal Times
I Have Felt Wonder. It may help if you add a short
definition of the word; in this case, moved by your
astonishment that what was before you could share
your world. List some incidents in which you experienced wonder. What comes to mind? Maybe it was
the time your dog had puppies. If you get an image,
stay with it, make it clearer and more vivid. Look at
the sights, smell the smells, hear the sounds. What were
you feeling, thinking, doing? Live that experience
again in your imagination.

If you have trouble coming up with a time when
you felt wonder, then you are shooting for too important an incident. Think of some *little* wonders and
try again: touching the foot of a newborn baby, stop-
ping on the sidewalk to admire the dew in a spider
web.

When you have relished the experience of wonder,
pick another heartwarming from the list and use it to
head another journal page and relive times when you
had this experience: The time you washed and ban-
daged your sister's scraped knee, *caring* so deeply for
her. The time you *delighted* in working with your
mother, preparing for a birthday party. The time you
responded sensitively to your girlfriend when she was
upset over having lost her job. Note that your heartwarming experiences were immediate benefits to you,
ends in themselves, not means to an end.

Practice 4

ENTER INTO A HEARTWARMING
EXPERIENCE

This practice goes well with the previous one. Sensi-
tized by reliving a past heartwarming experience, you
willfully put yourself into such an experience now,
with the events and circumstances of the moment.
Thus you take what you can learn from times you have

loved in the past to help you practice loving in the present.

Pick one of the heartwarming experiences from the list and walk into this experience now. When you have that experience, what thoughts do you have? Think those thoughts now. When you have that experience, how do you behave? What is your posture, your state of tension or relaxation? Behave that way now. How do you feel when you have that experience? Feel that way now.

Have patience and appreciation for whatever results from this practice. As you gain expertise, you will find the results more and more gratifying as you practice it again and again.

 ————————————————————————

Waiting for Something Worthy of Loving

Love means setting aside walls, fences, and unlocking doors, and saying YES. . . . *One can be in paradise by simply saying "yes" to this moment.*

EMMANUEL (PAT RODEGAST)

Some people would use the word *loving* for only those times when we feel overwhelmed by how lovable someone or something is. For example, Elizabeth Barrett Browning wrote:

> *Unless you can die when the dream is past—*
> *Oh, never call it loving.*

If you have ever felt this kind of love, treasure your memory—the awe, delight, and sensitivity. But do not cling to these past loves or they will shut off your loving now and in the future. Hold their memories as a taste of what your life might be like more of the time, with the events and people of today, not just with the few that overwhelmed you in the past.

These overwhelming loves can set a standard that keeps out *lesser* opportunities. You can get stuck in pictures of what loving *should* be like. Your friends and the popular media may agree with your expectations of how unusual something should be before you can love it. Do not limit the lovable to those few objects you deem *worthy* of loving, and thus define to be scarce. If you have lost your ability to love for these reasons, treasure the *little* experiences like attention, awareness, concern, interest, and liking as forms of love. The lovable is not scarce; it is everywhere. Your job is to see it that way.

The power of the word *loving* is enhanced, not reduced, by counting the *little* experiences as forms of love. You are living a *yes* whenever you open up and engage positively with the world. Of course, you certainly don't have to acknowledge the small experiences with a word as loaded as *love*. You can hold back, unwilling to delight fully, and wait for "the big one," for the person or event that will reach out and grab you. You can wait a long time for the big one—maybe even a lifetime. In the meanwhile, you will be ignoring the many little ones that are there all the time. Waiting to love something extraordinary keeps the extraordinary from sneaking into the ordinary. By loving the ordinary you make it extraordinary.

Practice 5

HOW HAS WAITING TO LOVE AFFECTED YOUR LIFE?

In this practice you think back over your life, while writing in your journal, asking how your life has been affected by waiting for something worthy of loving. What opportunities to experience the various heart-warmings of love have offered themselves to you while you held back because they did not seem right or because you were saving your loving until something better came along? With what boredom have you greeted the new day because you figured it was going to be just like yesterday? What flower has gone un-smelled, what person unkissed, what friend or relative unappreciated?

This practice is designed to let you see the power that your beliefs and attitudes have on your life. Your discoveries might make it easier for you to try out other beliefs and attitudes in order to love more.

Practice 6

WHEN HAVE YOU LOVED IN THE LAST TWENTY-FOUR HOURS?

The eye of love makes every person in the world friendly and attractive.

SAI BABA

What is the Godhead?
It is the passing of a bottle with all your soul.

ENKAN

In this practice you reflect back over this day and recall specific times you have loved—that is, responded to something in your life with a heartfelt yes. Focus on the moment, on the here and now. You may have been engrossed in a task, or paused to compliment a co-worker, or appreciated the bird singing outside your window. Look for the *little, ordinary* examples of loving and you will find them.

As your life grows richer in loving, this practice will become more and more an acknowledgment of your expertise. You will be able to shorten the time from twenty-four hours, eventually to an hour or less, and you will have many incidents to recall because you are naturally responding more lovingly.

List as many occasions as you can remember within the last twenty-four hours when you have loved. Take a minute to relive each one in your imagination. Enjoy your visualization, and pat yourself on the back for having turned that bit of your life into loving. Consult the list of heartwarmings for suggestions on what to look for.

Then, do the same practice for events in the last hour. This will require that you give up the belief that loving demands some rare, overwhelming experience.

Do the same practice, right now, for the events of the past ten seconds. This requires that you alternate between attending to the world with the strong intention of appreciating something, actually appreciating it, and writing down what you find.

The Objects of Love

True love is not a feeling by which we are overwhelmed. It is a committed, thoughtful decision.

M. SCOTT PECK

Love is a heartfelt yes you direct at something. That something is the object of your love. These objects may be yourself, other people, the world, places, things, sounds, sights, tastes, feelings, ideas, what you are doing, your life, the whole, God.

Cultivating the art of loving involves increasing the number of objects you are willing to love. Ultimately, you will increase this number beyond limit, and your experience will confirm your ability to love any object you choose.

Practice 7

WHAT IS IN YOUR LIFE TO LOVE?

Sixty-six times have these eyes beheld the changing scenes of Autumn.

I have said enough about moonlight,
  Ask me no more.
Only listen to the voice of pines and cedars, when no wind
  stirs.

                    RYO-NEN (HER LAST COMPOSITION)

The purpose of this practice is for you to realize, at any time, that the shower of riches available to love is greater than you could possibly do justice to.

Think through a typical day, week, and month to note every possible candidate for your loving—people, places, activities, animals. Ask yourself, What is in my life to love? Vary the question by replacing *love* with a verb form of one of the heartwarmings. For example: What is in my life to celebrate? To appreciate? What could I care for more deeply? What do I take for granted that I could be grateful for? What could I be more sensitive to?

Use this practice whenever you feel depressed or upset. Try it when you first wake up in the morning, while you are at work, driving the car, doing something you dislike, or lying sick in bed. From right where you are at the moment, list all the objects you are aware of that you could love. If convenient, write out your list. When you have finished that list, take a new sheet of paper and make a list five times as long that includes none of the first items.

If you find you cannot do this, you are limiting lovable objects to *big wonderful objects*. Instead, see *little wonderful objects* as lovable: the way the sunbeam reflects off the dust motes in the air, the touch of your clothing as it embraces your body, the smell of dinner, your dog's noseprints on the windows of your car, the sound of a friend's footsteps.

Prepare for a day or an activity by asking: What will be in my life today that I can love? You need no reason to love something except that you choose to care for it, to engage yourself deeply in it. Do this practice until you know in your bones that you could make this list

infinitely long, that you could do it even if you were
deaf or blind, if your mobility depended on a wheel-
chair or you were confined to a hospital bed.

Becoming an Expert Lover

Whatever your hand finds to do, do it with your might.
ECCLESIASTES

Love, love, love, that is the soul of genius.
WOLFGANG AMADEUS MOZART

Becoming an expert at loving is like becoming an expert
at any other complex skill. It takes practice born out of a
commitment to excel in the moment. One important skill
to practice is cultivating internal voices inside your mind
that do not obstruct but empower you in loving. In the next
chapter, we will address the first of such voices—a set of
common beliefs about loving that block people's progress.
Once you see them for what they are, as myths rather than
truths, you will be able to challenge them rather than act
on them, and replace them by beliefs that make loving easier.

After the final "No" comes a "Yes."
On that yes the future of the world depends.
WALLACE STEVENS

2 ❦ NINE MYTHS OF LOVING

Man is made by his belief. As he believes, so he is.

BHAGAVAD GITA

We are born believing. A man bears beliefs as a tree bears apples.

RALPH WALDO EMERSON

Y ou are made by your beliefs. As a human, you learned your nature from the society into which you were born. A major role of any society is to teach children a set of basic beliefs—what is real, what is important, what is possible, and who they are in the scheme of things. With these beliefs you build your reality, your values, your realm of possibilities, and your sense of self. To sustain your beliefs, you habitually accept as true the internal voices that speak them. You act as if they were true, thus limiting the options available to you to the ones the system allows.

When you notice how different these beliefs can be from one person or group to the next, you realize that what is common to all of us is not the content of any particular set of beliefs. It is, rather, that we all have *some* set of basic beliefs that we *know* to be true. We live our lives consistent with these beliefs, as if we were in a powerful trance, cast on us by our society as we move through infancy into adulthood—and cast by us onto future generations.

Your basic beliefs reinforce themselves because, when you live your life in accordance with them, you continually reconfirm their truth. A self-confirming belief is not something that you are aware you believe, but something you simply know to be true. An example is knowing that it is more important to be loved than to love. As you approach life while taking for granted the truth of this internal voice, whenever the world seems not to be giving you the love you demand, you will upset yourself about it. So, over and over, your experience will confirm your belief. Unknown to you, however, you could easily confirm the contradictory voice that says to love is most important and that lovable people are everywhere—if only that voice were strong enough for you to hear and act upon.

You sustain most patterns in your behavior by a set of such beliefs. When you see how they work, you might call them myths. But when you are unaware, you just accept them as the way things are. To increase the loving in your life, you need to explore and challenge the voices about loving that you now take for granted. Then you will need to develop new love-enhancing voices to replace the old ones that get in the way, and to bolster each new belief by selectively remembering experiences that confirm it rather than the old belief. In time, you will live from a set of love-enhancing beliefs that you confirm each day in experience.

The Myth of Romance

> *All which we behold*
> *Is full of blessings.*
> WILLIAM WORDSWORTH

To many people, the word *loving* means only powerful romantic or sexual attraction. Under the best of circumstances, such attraction is so strong as to sweep you into the most heartfelt *yes* experience of your life. Yet so often, once you taste this experience, you lose it. Circumstances or your beloved may break off your relationship, your beloved's less desirable features may keep you from sustaining your love, or you may simply lack the will and the skill to turn an ongoing relationshp into intense loving.

The myth of romance says that romantic attraction is the only real loving, and if you want to love, you must keep looking for the *right* person who will ignite in you an over-whelming *yes* reaction. Thus you live in the dream of ro-mantic love—searching and hoping, with bursts of op-timism and excitement and long periods of frustration and discouragement. The myth of romance says you have no other choice.

It is easy to see how romance and sex might, and ideally would, involve love—a heartfelt yes toward another person and toward your own body. But lots of us know from personal experience, and the media never let us forget, that romance and sex can spring from biology, boredom, ego-tism, fantasy, anger, or frustration as easily as they can spring from love.

The romantic and sexual areas of life offer the possibility of making love, but they also offer the possibility of merely "making out." You need skills to take romantic relation-ships past fantasies and mechanics and turn them into lovemaking—how to be sensitive to this person, to respond to him or her, to delight in him or her in every imaginable way, and to sustain this love and build on it as you create the shared memories of a long-term relationship.

If you are not blinded by the romantic myth, you can use each romantic relationship, even those that do not look like "the right one," to love as intensely as you can. Beyond that, you can use all the other arenas in your life to practice loving, confident that the skills you acquire will carry over into your romantic life. Thus you will experience love in all your activities and will improve your skill at filling them all with love.

The myth of romantic love is an example of the myth that there is only one arena for loving. As you go through life, you may be tempted many times to embrace this myth, to identify something special that you *need* to love. For example, if you have no children or want more, you might tell yourself that only in raising children can you really love. When your children leave home, you might say that the loving period of your life is over. When you lose or give up any cherished part of your life, such as your home, your health, a friend or relative, a pet, your job, or your independence, you might assert that you will never really love again.

Such myths confirm themselves—if you believe one and live your life from its truth, you will experience love only within that single arena. If you deny these myths and practice loving in all arenas, you will find that you live in a rich and lovable world.

Practice 8

HOW HAS THE MYTH OF ROMANCE AFFECTED YOUR LIFE?

For each of the nine myths discussed in this chapter, a valuable practice consists of thinking over your life, while writing in your journal, exploring the role that this myth has played in your loving. In some cases you will vividly recall how a belief has kept you from loving. In some cases you will realize that you have never believed the myth or that you believed it in the past but no longer do. The purpose of these practices is for you to replace the internal voices that sustain these myths with contradictory voices that empower, rather than restrict your ability to love.

In this practice you think over your life, while writing in your journal, asking what role romance has played in your loving. Is your loving primarily restricted to romantic/sexual relationships, or to non-romantic experiences, or is this an issue for you? Remember times you loved someone or something that had nothing to do with romance—relatives and

pets, teddy bears, books, music, playing ball, the sound
of rain on the roof. How willing are you now to love
intensely someone or something that holds no romantic interest?

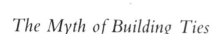

The Myth of Building Ties

What is the Way?
   Lovely flowers open by the mossy roadside;
   The green willows dance in the spring breezes.
                                          RAKAN

I remember having tea with friends one spring afternoon
in 1967 in an old house in Oxford. I was looking out onto
the yard just as the sun was casting its last rays. Suddenly
two foxes tumbled out of the bushes in a playful chase.
They leaped and danced and sped across the lawn in a blaze
of energy and then were gone. I built no ties with them; I
never saw them again. But I loved them then and I love
them now, and I will always treasure them.

You build ties with a person, animal, place, or object as
you share your life with it over a period of time. Through
shared activities you build a store of memories that bind
your life with the other. Your relationship with the other
exists in your memories; how loving your relationships are
depends on how positively you interpret these memories.

In a loving life you build and maintain many loving relationships. But the myth of building ties says that if you
want to love anything, you must forge ties to it over periods
of time. The myth requires you to take the time to build
the ties of a relationship whenever you sense that love might
be possible. It implies that "I love you" means "let us spend
time together and create the shared memories of a relationship."

You can work to develop as many long-term relationships as you want and have time to care for. But the belief that loving demands entangling the loved one in your future will make you afraid to love. You might feel torn at the thought of loving one person if you also love someone else. You might refuse to delight in an activity that you have little time to practice. In truth, you can love endlessly, while you choose to cultivate relationships with relatively few of the objects of your love.

The extreme form of the myth of building ties is the belief that true love is love that never ends. If you love someone now, you must always love that person. Your lives must be permanently entangled, "until death do you part." You must build ties forever.

With family members, some friends, careers, pets, and hobbies, it pays to keep building positive relationships indefinitely, to commit to doing so, and to work hard at it. The payoff is obvious. But just because sustaining love through time is desirable is no reason to demand it in order for love to be deemed true. That sets up a test for true love: Can you sustain this experience for the next fifty years?

The myth of building ties forever is especially cruel to those in pain. When your marriage or other deep relationship is ending by any cause other than death, this myth may lead you to trash the riches in your memory. Since you did not stay together forever, "it didn't turn out," so it must not have been real love.

The myth of building ties forever blackmails you into downplaying the delights of the moment by pressuring you to sustain those delights into the future. No one can be confident of doing that. Of course you don't know what the future will bring. Whatever it brings, it will bring you plenty to love, even if it is not this particular loved one. So love *this*, right now, without reference to the future. Whenever you experience the heartwarmings of love, that is real love, true love, as real as love gets. Tomorrow you may be loving something else, but now you are loving this.

Practice 9

HOW HAS THE MYTH OF BUILDING TIES AFFECTED YOUR LIFE?

In this practice you think over your life, while writing in your journal, asking how you have used relationship or its lack in your life. Do you typically love only when you create an ongoing relationship with your love object, or do you shy away from building relationships and see them only as entanglements? Are there certain areas, such as romance, where the myth of building ties forever plays a large role, while in other areas you are willing to delight in something and move on?

Remember times you have been deeply moved by events you could not possibly form relationships with, such as seeing a sunset, hearing a piece of music, or eating a meal. How willing are you to love intensely and never see the object of your love again? Recall times when you have loved something or someone deeply, knowing that the relationship would soon end.

Remember other times when you declined to open up and appreciate something or someone because you knew a permanent relationship was impossible. When have you used the myth of building ties forever to devalue the heartwarmings of love after you found that the relationship with your loved one had ended? How willing are you to give up this myth and stop worrying about what the future will bring regarding an appropriate love object and simply love it?

The Myth of Being Loved

Don't worry about whether other people are loving you. That's their problem.

KEN KEYES, JR.

May it be, O Lord, that I seek not so much to be consoled as to console, to be understood as to understand, to be loved as to love; because it is in giving oneself that one receives; it is in forgetting oneself that one is found.

ST. FRANCIS OF ASSISI

It is easy to believe the myth of being loved—that what is really important is not to love, but to be loved and approved by others. There is the usual measure of truth to the myth. Certainly, in order for you to have good romantic or business relationships, someone had better think well of you. People have an inborn desire to be loved, appreciated, and respected by those around them. It is useful and satisfying to receive love. But it is better for you to love than to be loved.

After all, it is the lover rather than the loved one who has the heartwarming experiences. The loved one is at most a stimulus and often just a lucky beneficiary. The lover is the artist who takes that stimulus and paints awe or celebration out of it. Lovers do not need to have their value affirmed by others—they know the value of their lives through their loving experiences.

Furthermore, you cannot directly control how people respond to you. Often they do not actually respond to you, but to old memories you innocently trigger. But you can do something about loving—practice it, experience it, live in it.

Part of the myth of being loved is the myth of acknowledgment, the belief that love is valid only when communicated to someone who acknowledges and appreciates it. Yet think of a time when you were moved by beauty; for example, when you watched the sun rise and felt at one with a universe that has put you on a such a lovely planet. Did you have to tell someone about your experience in order to validate it, or paint a picture or take a photo of the sunrise in order to ratify your awe and wonder?

If someone accepts your love, that person is showing his

or her love for you, not passing you on a test to validate your love. Love cannot be validated—the experience is all the validation there can be. Nor can anyone invalidate it, unless you do so yourself. You do not need others to ratify your experiences. If you pour loving energy into the world through your work and your business goes broke, that does not make your energy less loving. If your neighbors see only the weeds and not the flowers in your garden, that does not affect the care with which you planted your seeds.

Practice 10

HOW HAS THE MYTH OF BEING LOVED AFFECTED YOUR LIFE?

> *Yes: The young sparrows*
> *If you treat them tenderly—*
> *Thank you with droppings.*
>
> ISSA

In this practice you think over your life, while writing in your journal, asking how much you have sought to be loved and how much you have been willing to love without worrying about whether others loved you back. How willing are you to commit to loving intensely without concern for whether others love you back? Do you typically seek to gain approval, applause, and admiration, or to experience enthusiasm, joy, and wonder, or both? When you have been loved or applauded, how satisfying has it been?

The Myth of Agreement

I have given each being a separate and unique way of seeing and knowing and saying that knowledge. What seems wrong to you is right for him. What is poison to one is honey to someone else.

RUMI (SAID AS A QUOTE OF GOD)

As I was growing up, and afterward when I returned home, Mother and I washed the dishes after meals. She washed and I dried. Our dishwashing often turned into verbal sparring matches: "This fork's still dirty, you didn't wash it." "Sure I washed it. The person drying dishes is supposed to catch those things and wash it himself." Dad worried when we did this. He believed that love meant agreement, never bickering. Yet, I would give a lot right now to be at the kitchen sink arguing with Mother!

Dad, like many people, believed you should agree with someone you love. After all, love is a heartfelt yes. Yet loving someone means directing a yes toward the *person*, not toward that person's ideas or behavior. Your love is your private, positive experience, not a positive statement or action. You can love someone and disagree with her, even vigorously. You can love her and still say no, even a loud and dramatic no.

If you feel you must agree with anyone you love, then you will become a doormat and attract people who are looking for a place to wipe their feet. Indeed, in order to cultivate the experience of *yes*, you must be able to say no, to speak up calmly for your own convictions, without fearing it will threaten the love. To do that demands that you not confuse love with agreement—they are not the same.

Granted, you do not want to start overwhelming your partner with disagreements. He or she may get puzzled, upset, and even decide to look to more agreeable partners for a relationship. So, explain that you are not yet skillful at gracefully asserting yourself; ask your partner's support.

An extreme form of the myth of agreement is believing that if you love someone, you should *submit* to him, do what he wants you to do. The costs of submission are even greater than those of agreement. You attract partners who want someone to dominate because they are insecure in relating to people as equals. You stifle your growth and prevent yourself from pouring into the world the unique energy that is yours.

If you think that loving requires you to abandon your values and give yourself away, you are not likely to do a lot of loving. You can love someone and refuse to give him what he wants, even when he pleads with you in a most moving way. You do not need to support or nurture someone in order to love him. It is always your choice to do it or not do it.

The time to say yes is when both your head and your heart freely say yes. If you are not free to agree or disagree, no matter how deeply you love someone, then what you call the experience of love will be more like slavery. The myth of agreement has led many people to live their romantic lives in slavery. The same holds when someone else submits to you. If the person who loves you is not free to agree or disagree with you, to do or not do what you want, then that person is not your beloved but your slave.

If you are in a relationship in which there is a demand for agreement or submission, do not blame anyone. Communicate your determination to be together in freedom, and solicit similar determination from your partner. Get support from books, friends, a group, or a counselor. It is never too late to learn to be free.

 ——————————————————————————

Practice 11

HOW HAS THE MYTH OF AGREEMENT AFFECTED YOUR LIFE?

In this practice you think over your life, while writing in your journal, asking what role the myth of agreement has played. Do you feel obliged to agree with or submit to someone you love, or to have that person agree with or submit to you? Do you believe that disagreement has to be nasty and angry, rather than calm and loving? What has been the cost of this myth to your relationships?

How willing are you to love deeply without automatically doing what your loved one wants, or expecting that your loved one behaves as you want? Which of your relationships might be jeopardized if each person practiced calmly asking for what he or she wanted instead of submitting or dominating?

Practice 12

SAY NO WITH LOVE

In this practice you let disagreement enter your loving relationships. When you disagree with someone or say no, consciously practice keeping your heart open in a yes. Let that person know that you are doing this in order to express yourself and to grow as an individual and in the relationship. Explain that through this practice you intend to improve not only your loving but also your communication, since it is hard to say no without becoming angry or judgmental. Urge your partner to join you, so you support each other in this venture. Then practice calmly speaking and standing up for what you think, even if you disagree.

Observe yourself closely when you say no. Do you close yourself off from others? Do you prepare to defend yourself? Does your heart race or pound, your palms sweat, your stomach churn?

Whenever you notice you are about to say no—to turn down a request, to correct or reprimand someone—resolve to say no clearly and to appreciate and respect the other person. Then communicate your no, while feeling love in your heart. If you have already said no and closed off your feelings, then immediately open up again and approve of the other person as a person. This is simply someone who has asked of you what you are unwilling to grant, or who has done something you are unwilling to approve of. See if saying no when no is called for makes it easier to say yes later.

The Myth of Pain

Restore me with raisins, comfort me with apples: for I am sick with love.

OLD TESTAMENT, SONG OF SOLOMON

The myth of pain says that if you love you will be hurt, badly hurt. Too many people have experienced so much pain in connection with the people they most loved—parents, siblings, friends, lovers, would-be lovers, spouses, children—that they automatically associate loving with pain. They have been abandoned, abused, and disappointed by the people they loved, not just once, but over and over again. If you associate pain with loving, you will challenge the truth of the old expression, "Better to have loved and lost than never to have loved at all."

But pain is inevitable in human life, more so if you pull away from love than if you move into it. Since it was the big loves that led to your pain, in order to break free of this myth, embrace the little loves that can fill up your life. Do not worry about the big ones for a while. Your protective instincts have no reason to concern themselves about enthusiasm for your garden or your enjoyment of tonight's dinner. As you exercise the little loves, work to make peace with your past, and replace the myths that get in the way, the familiar tie between love and pain will fade away.

 ————————————————————————

Practice 13

HOW HAS THE MYTH OF PAIN AFFECTED YOUR LIFE?

In this practice you think over your life, while writing in your journal, asking to what extent you have associated loving with pain. What past events have linked these two concepts in your mind? What times have you held back your love for fear of the pain you felt must inevitably follow?

When else have you loved when you did not experience pain, but joy instead? Recall as many of these events as possible. Are you willing to stop recalling only the painful times, and instead begin to recall your most wonderful loving experiences?

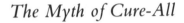

The Myth of Cure-All

> So instead of getting to Heaven, at last—
> I'm going, all along.
>
> EMILY DICKINSON

The myth of cure-all says that the wonders of finding the right loved one will transform your life, solve your problems, end your loneliness, cure your ills, and give your life meaning and security. There is just enough truth in this myth to make it seem reasonable, except that it directs your attention the wrong way.

There is no question about love having the power to solve problems, end loneliness, transform lives, and give them meaning and security. It is true that a new romantic partner, a new baby, or the job you wanted might be all the stimulus you need to react with transforming love—at least for a while.

But the myth of cure-all approaches loving backward, from the outside rather than the inside. The very notion of a cure-all would attract you only if you were unhappy with your present life and look to the future rather than the present for something positive. The myth sends you out to change the circumstances in your life to something so positive you cannot help but react positively. That approach has little chance of long-term success, even if once in a while you are lucky enough to find such a wonderful stimulus.

The way to experience security in love is to embark on the path of loving and develop, over time, the ability to love whomever and whatever you are confronting. That path does indeed transform your life, but it happens because you make it happen, regardless of circumstances, rather than because you have been lucky enough to find some rare, ideal loved one.

Practice 14

HOW HAS THE MYTH OF CURE-ALL AFFECTED YOUR LIFE?

In this practice you think over your life, while writing in your journal, asking to what extent you have felt that finding the right loved one would solve all your problems and transform your life. The cure-all might be a romantic partner, but it also might be a job or a house or a baby. When you have achieved this beloved goal, how did your experience fit your expectations? To what extent have you resisted loving objects that you felt sure did not have the power to transform your life? Are you willing to love intensely even objects you know offer no cure-all, and see where your progress on the path of loving will take you?

The Myth of Action

A spark of pure love is more precious before God . . . than all the other works taken together, even if, according to appearances, one does nothing.

ST. JOHN OF THE CROSS

The myth of action says that in order to love you must act in a way that serves your loved one. Yet you can base service on any number of experiences other than love—for example, on fear, martyrdom, guilt, expectation, or greed. No one can tell from looking at your behavior whether you are loving. Loving actions are fallout from the internal yes on which they are based. It pays to distinguish between the experience of loving and the behavior of a loving action.

Of course, your actions affect your experience. You can deliberately act so as to further your loving, and you can love in order to make your actions more effective. But you do not have to *do* anything in order to love. If you love someone, you are not responsible for that person's welfare. Doing something for someone else's welfare comes from your own choice, from social agreements, and from commitments you choose to make. One of the many considerations that leads you to make such commitments is likely to be your love.

 ────────────────────────────────

Practice 15

HOW HAS THE MYTH OF ACTION AFFECTED YOUR LIFE?

In this practice you think over your life, while writing in your journal, asking to what extent you have felt that you had to *do* something to express any love that you experience. When have you refused to love because you did not want to do anything about it? When has the grudging nature of your loving actions sapped you of the experience of love? Are you willing to distinguish loving actions from the experience of loving, with your actions always being a choice that you are free either to make or not make?

 ────────────────────────────────

The Myth of Spontaneity

> *Dig a well before you are thirsty.*
> CHINESE PROVERB

The myth of spontaneity says that real love must be spontaneous, never practiced or rehearsed. It says that if you plan in advance to love, your experience will be mechanical, artificial, and false. Life is indeed delightful when it surprises you with an unexpected treasure that you can spontaneously cherish. The trouble arises when you believe that to be the *only* way you can love.

In this, practicing loving resembles playing baseball or the piano. Of course you want to perform each activity freshly and spontaneously, in response to the circumstances and feelings of the moment. Yet practicing music and sports makes you better at being spontaneous and fresh when you perform. Planning a party or picnic does not keep it from being fun. It is no different with loving.

Practicing sets the habit of loving in diverse circumstances. Life contains some surprises that are less than delightful—loss, error, disappointment, failure, pain, illness, loneliness, aging—all of which are inevitable challenges to your skill at loving. By thinking through such challenges in advance, you will be less likely to get caught up in their drama when they happen.

You may crave the adventure of an unplanned life, and so dismiss planning or practicing as taking away life's charm or value. Believing the myth of spontaneity will make you resist the ideas and practices of this book—you will not prepare in advance to love, you will not practice the skills of loving. The years will fly by and you will still be waiting for the few especially delightful surprises that the world offers you.

 ———————————————————————

Practice 16

HOW HAS THE MYTH OF SPONTANEITY AFFECTED YOUR LIFE?

The purpose of this practice is for you to commit to the regular practice of loving because you recognize how much it has cost you to wait for it to happen spontaneously.

Think over your life, while writing in your journal, asking what role spontaneity or rehearsal and preparation have played. When you open up to the world in loving, do you do so spontaneously or only when you are well rehearsed? What has been the cost in your life of not preparing to love in advance, of not practicing loving? Are you willing to practice loving regularly in order to love more?

The Myth of Difficulty

The work is easy and the medicine is not far away. If the secret is disclosed, it will be so simple that everyone may get a good laugh.

CHANG PO-TUAN

The myth of difficulty says that the world is unkind, life is hard, it ends in death, and you are lucky if you manage to slip even a few little snippets of loving into your life. Believe this and you will certainly confirm it, since you will be defeated in loving without even trying.

Yet the joy of rich, intense loving is your human birthright. You have, unfortunately, been taught to put other activities first. When you were a child, your teachers spent years teaching you arithmetic, but no one mentioned loving. As an adult, you learned to work productively, even to raise children, but you had no teachers of loving.

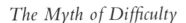

As in learning music or art, learning to love life demands a good coach and a lot of practice. Debunk the myths that do not work and learn new rules of thumb that do. In music, art, and sports you know lots of people who became experts through work and practice, not because they were born that way. Their example shows you how a high level of commitment pays off. You may not know many experts on loving, so it may seem to be harder. It is not. Just as the expert pianist can sit down at any time and play exquisitely, eventually all it will take for you to love is to decide to.

 ────────────────────────────────

Practice 17

HOW HAS THE MYTH OF DIFFICULTY AFFECTED YOUR LIFE?

In this practice you think over your life, while writing in your journal, asking how difficult you have felt it was to love. When has it been easy to love? When has it been most difficult? When have you given up on loving because you knew it was unlikely or impossible? What has the myth of difficulty cost you?

 ────────────────────────────────

This chapter has addressed beliefs that can block people from loving. We next consider how people actually do love.

The greatest discovery of any generation is that human beings can alter their lives by altering their attitudes of mind.

ALBERT SCHWEITZER

3 ❦ REACTIVE AND INTENTIONAL LOVING

We do not see things as they are, but as we are.

TALMUD

The inside always manifests itself on the outside.
ANCIENT CHINESE PROVERB QUOTED BY CONFUCIUS

Experience—As You Interpret It

We imagine that our mind is a mirror, that it is more or less accurately reflecting what is happening outside us. On the contrary, our mind itself is the principal element of creation.

RABINDRANATH TAGORE

Most people hold the view that human experience is an automatic reaction to physical circumstances. Your senses seem simply to mirror what is happening, independent of your will. When people around you appear to experience things the same way you do, this supports your belief that human experience reflects reality. It seems obvious that there is only one reality, so, given your circumstances, your experience is the only one you could possibly have.

In the combination of event and person that leads to experience, the reactive view focuses solely on the event. It ignores the person whose interpretation of the event creates the experience—the person who *demands* that this incident should not have happened, who *decides* that the present situation is uninteresting, who *judges* the threat to be awful or too painful, who *evaluates* this object as special or attractive and therefore *pays attention* only to its attractive features. Experience is not a mirror. The people around you seem to experience things the same way you do not because that is the only way they can be experienced, but because they share your culture and learned to interpret events in similar ways.

Through selective attention and constant interpretation, you transform circumstances into experience; this is how you *create* experience. Everyone must interpret life somehow, and there is no right way to do it. The fact is, the world is not intrinsically *any* way. There are as many realities as there are people who are willing and able to interpret their circumstances differently. It is not given to us to know the nature of whatever real world might lie beyond our interpretations.

The path of loving is a path on which you consciously choose how to create your experience. Suppose, for example, you are standing on a busy street and a man steps on your foot as he walks by. Your foot hurts, but you quickly dismiss it as the pain goes away. "After all, it was an accident, and the street *is* crowded."

But suppose you are standing on the same street and a man with a wicked gleam in his eye comes over, stomps on your foot, and then walks away. Even as the pain fades away, what is your response? "The rotten jerk! He shouldn't have done that!" You experience more than just a painful toe, and more than an event that is not the way you want it to be. You experience an event that *should not have happened*, and because of your dramatic interpretation, you may still be angry hours later.

If you *accept the reality* of a stomped foot in a world that has one footstomper for every ten thousand people, you get some physical pain and maybe frustration and regret. If you *demand* that the world not be the way it is and condemn the stomper by dramatizing how wrong he was, you get anger and resentment in addition. Thus does interpretation create experience.

Just because you create your own experience does not imply that you can ignore or wish away the circumstances to create different ones. The pain of a stomped foot is yours no matter what. The circumstances of life are the raw material that you attend to and interpret in order to create your experiences. Since your habits and beliefs keep getting in the way of testing the limits, you can never be sure how raw that raw material is.

Practice 18

LISTEN TO OTHERS INTERPRET EVENTS

Men are not moved by things but by the view which they take of them.

EPICTETUS

In this practice you study the power of interpretation and selective attention in people's lives. You see different people interpret and thus experience the *same* events in dramatically different ways. You cultivate the role of a witness, one who is just noticing and not entering into the particular drama at hand. The ability to move into this witness position will help you on your loving path.

Listen to others, in person and in the media, as they interpret life according to the reactive view. Their circumstances seem so obviously to cause their experiences—they must find the good, avoid the bad, and control or change what happens. Notice that they get angry or upset because something happens they think should not; they get bored because nearby events are not interesting; they get frightened if something too painful or unpleasant occurs; they can love only the most attractive objects or people.

Notice also people whose lives are consumed by their selective attention to traumatic events from their past, such as an assault, a failure, or a loss; or by features of their body, like its appearance or agility. Noticing means neither agreeing nor disagreeing with their interpretations. The point is simply to *see* the role of interpretations and how many different ones are possible.

You may not be used to listening to the interpretations going on in your mind—they play out so automatically—but they are there. As you grew up, you formed a set of standard interpretations ready for all kinds of events, and they flash into your mind at a moment's notice.

Perhaps, when you were young, your mother growled "miserable creep!" at someone crowding her out in traffic; now, as an adult, when someone cuts in front of you, you know that you have been victimized by a miserable creep. You may not remember your mother's remark or think of yourself as judging or interpreting. The person clearly *is* a miserable creep. The similar event triggers the old interpretations, and the anger floods in. Thus, because the interpretation is so automatic and obvious, you seem to confirm experimentally the reactive view that events cause experience.

Practice 19

LISTEN TO YOUR INTERNAL VOICES

Remember: You are not the chatter that you hear in your head; you are the hearer of that chatter.

BILL HARVEY

You express most of your interpretations in internal voices you probably call thoughts. In this practice, you simply attend to those voices and listen to them in much the same way you listen to a radio. This will enhance your understanding of how talkative and convincing your internal voices are, and it will also give you a place from which to listen, where you can just witness or observe these voices rather than be run by them.

Whenever it is convenient—for example, as you work, drive, walk, eat, or prepare for bed—pay attention to the voices inside your head. Do not label them or change them or change what you are doing. Simply listen to the chatter. Come to know each voice; study it, as you would study a new houseguest. What judgments does it make? What tone does it take—harsh or kindly? How much time does it dwell on events from the past, events that may happen in the future, or on events happening now? How does it treat you —with care, support, and love, or with criticism, self-doubt, and sarcasm?

Practice 20

ATTEND WITHOUT INTERPRETATION

All hangs on your faith in yourself, on the conviction that what you see and hear, think and feel is real. Why not question this faith?

SRI NISARGADATTA MAHARAJ

What can you say about people who don't see what they're staring at?

KABIR

People rarely realize how much time they spend interpreting whatever they are attending to by judging, evaluating, analyzing, and comparing. In this practice you experience afresh, focusing without any interpretation at all. This will strengthen your ability to direct your attention, and it will give you some experiences of how startlingly new an object can be when unencumbered by the usual load of mental chatter. It will let you recognize the powerful role the verbal chatter in your mind plays in your life.

Pick an object and simply look at it attentively, without any verbal interpretation, for a predetermined period of time. If you hear an internal voice—for example, saying how interesting or dull this is, how nice or ugly, how much you like or dislike one of its features, how it compares with something else, what a stupid practice this is—just notice the voice and let go of it. Then put your attention back on what you are looking at.

Extend this same practice to listening to something afresh—perhaps to birdsong, traffic noise, kids playing, a clock ticking, or music. Just listen to the sounds, with no interpretation at all.

Extend this practice to your sense of touch—perhaps to petting your cat or dog, feeling the bedclothes or blankets when you are in bed, the sun or the breeze, the water in a bath or shower. Do the same with taste and smell.

If you are unpracticed at this or other forms of meditation, you are likely to be surprised at the strength of your internal voice and at how hard it is to shut it up. That internal voice injects your habits of inattention and interpretation into every potentially fresh experience, often overpowering your senses so you hardly know what you are seeing or hearing. All you hear is the chatter.

You may also be surprised at how much you enjoy these experiences with no interpretation of any sort. It is enough just to see, hear, feel, and taste.

 ———————————————————

Reactive Loving

The lover is looking in a mirror in which he is beholding his Self.
PLATO

The reactive view of loving implies that in order to evoke delight, a person, object, or event must be unusually delightful. The myth of reactive love holds that to be lovable, something must be especially attractive. You can enjoy paintings by Van Gogh, but not paintings by your neighbor. You could be charmed by a well-bred, healthy puppy, but not the scraggly mutt that appears at your door.

You may of course *fall* in love, have the experience of being helplessly propelled toward a beloved due to forces beyond your control. But how often does that happen, and how long does it last? What are you going to do with yourself while you wait around for the right one to show up?

Listen to the people around you and in the media. Notice how, in order to love more, they must control the world so they are surrounded by positive circumstances. Notice how they search for especially lovable objects, cling to those they find, try to get more of them, change them to make them better, or exchange them for different ones. If they find they cannot re-create the experience of loving, they try to relive it through their memories.

When you know only reactive loving, you have few tools for loving more. Your loving depends on the world providing the unusually lovable people or objects you can appreciate. These are, by definition, uncommon, so you will live in a world in which the lovable is scarce. You will spend your life seeking for the few that exist, and when you find one you will cling tightly to it for fear it will leave. Most of the time, rather than feel you have choices in your life, you will feel stuck with what the world offers you.

Since others must be *special* for you to love them, you also must be special if others are to love you. Chances are you are an ordinary human being, much like everyone else. In truth, there is nothing ordinary or special in the world. *Ordinary* and *special* are labels to stick on something to justify ignoring or appreciating it. You can see the specialness in anything. Loving breaks down the distinctions between ordinary and special and sees how wonderful it is to be a typical human being living among other typical humans and innumerable other creatures on what is probably a typical planet going around a typical star.

Rest assured that on a path of loving you will still have preferences, will distinguish between what you want and what you do not want, and will make choices as you go through life. Indeed, choosing one thing over another is easier on a path of loving because there is less at risk— whatever direction you choose to go, you will surely find much to love.

Practice 21

FIND YOUR REASONS FOR LIKING AND DISLIKING

Experience is not what happens to a man. It is what a man does with what happens to him.

ALDOUS HUXLEY

Everything has both positive and negative features. When you love something, you focus on the positive and let the negative be. When you dislike something, you bolster the negative and downplay the positive. In this practice you call to mind both positive and negative features and see how selective attention and interpretation work in creating experience. It will also strengthen your power to aim your attention and interpret what you find willfully.

Think of people you like or love now or have loved in the past. Head pages in your journal with their names and make two columns for each person. Down the left column list as many reasons as you can for loving this person. What attractive or positive features caused you to delight in or appreciate him or her? If you have difficulty pinpointing such reasons, speculate on what they might be. Also list, down the right column, as many unattractive or negative features of the person as you can think of. If you have trouble thinking of the latter, put down negative features that other people see or might see in this person, regardless of whether you see them yourself. Ask yourself, "If someone disliked this person, what might the reasons be?"

Do this practice for other people, animals, places, activities, and objects that you have liked and disliked. Especially good choices are ones that you once loved and later "fell out of love with," or that you once disliked and later learned to love.

Notice that, as you have chosen to love some of these and dislike others, someone else might either love or dislike any of them, simply by focusing on one list of features and not taking the other features seriously. One by one, consider the lists of features of the objects that you disliked, and imagine what it would be like to love that object. Would you be *willing* to love it? If not, why not?

Intentional Loving

> *The real orchards and fruits are within the heart; the reflection of their beauty is falling upon this water and earth (the external world). . . .*
>
> *All the deceived ones come to gaze on this reflection in the opinion that this is the place of Paradise.*
>
> *They are fleeing from the origins of the orchards; they are making merry over a phantom.*
>
> RUMI

Because loving means interpreting events with a yes, the role of interpretation in creating love becomes clear. The heartwarming experiences listed in Chapter 1 are alive with positive interpretations, each a bit different from the others. You *create* your loving by breathing a yes into objects and events in your life.

Of course, you can sustain the reactive view of loving. Suppose you are going along, living your life, when you happen to be attracted to someone. Her features seem so wonderful that you react with caring, delight, or wonder. As a reactive lover, when you notice that you are loving, you know what caused it—obviously the attractive features of your beloved.

What really happened was this: Your attention is always wandering here and there, depending on events. In this case, when you notice her fine features, they seem so wonderful that they surpass your standards or expectations, so you focus on them and aim at appreciating and caring for her. You have discovered her to be lovable. You actively scan her qualities for the positive, the beautiful, the awe-inspiring. As you find these, you reinforce your delight and joy, and she seems even better than before. You fall in love, into a whirlpool of positive interpretations, and you call the reasons for your love the fine features you first noticed, or the ones you found as you actively appreciated her.

But these reasons are not enough to *sustain* love, as countless people have found when they "fell out of love" with someone whose qualities remained steadfastly the same. As these people saw the inevitable negative aspects of their beloved more and more clearly, they became victims of a similar whirlpool in which they actively scanned for more negative features instead of positive. And, of course, they found them: new reasons to bolster a growing heartfelt no, directed at the former beloved.

The real reason for love is aiming to love—coming to the beloved with an open heart, determined to pay attention and appreciate. Most of us let our attention drift, restlessly seeking circumstances interesting enough to hold it for a moment before it goes on to something else. Our attention is a victim of circumstances, a boat adrift on the sea of life, and any loving we experience is reactive loving.

It need not be that way. You do not have to let your attention float or drop old interpretations onto today's events. You can *choose what you will love and choose to interpret it positively*, and thus love intentionally, rather than wait for the occasional flash of reactive loving. This enhances its value as the object of your love. Loving is no delusion; it is an artistic creation. Artists do not duplicate reality; they paint it, but by doing so they make it important in human life.

You can live in love, in a constant willingness to appreciate and delight in whatever is in your life. Heartwarming experiences flow from that intention; the circumstances just give you the excuse. The world is a screen onto which you project your love. And that is great news. Willfully responding with a yes opens a way of knowing the world that is always available. At *this* moment, you can choose to love. Now! After all, anything that might happen sometime in the future never happens at all unless it finally happens in some moment of *now*. Just as apathy, anger, or fear will spiral into ever greater intensity if you let it run, so will your heartfelt yes.

Practice 22

CHOOSE HOW YOU INTERPRET EVERYDAY ACTIVITIES

Happiness and love are just a choice away.
LEO BUSCAGLIA

You spend most of your life doing everyday things—washing dishes, taking a shower, driving the car, cooking or eating meals. You can interpret these activities in countless ways, and in this practice you choose to view what you are doing as expressions of love or as resented obligations. This will increase your awareness of how you create an experience. It will strengthen your skill at choosing your own interpretation rather than applying one automatically. It will make you less prone to embracing as obvious and inevitable the first interpretation that comes to mind.

Pick a commonplace activity and figure out how you would explain or describe it as an expression of loving. Take notes on your thoughts, or write out your description in your journal. Then take the same activity, only this time explain or describe it as a resented duty. If possible, tell your descriptions to at least one friend, putting strong feeling into each description.

For example, you can wash the dishes as a service to your family, the people you love, or as a celebration of food, plenty, and loved ones, or as an exercise in efficiency, or as a time to meditate, either in silence or with music, or as an opportunity to do one of the practices in this book. On the other hand, you could see dishwashing as a miserable, tiring chore that takes up valuable time you can't spare and that leaves your hands white and pasty. Besides, the dishes will get dirty again within an hour!

Then, whenever you actually perform the activity, use your internal voice to alternate between the two interpretations. See how powerfully you can put yourself into each view; sincerely believe what you are telling yourself. Notice that the activity does not dictate any right view to take of it. Clean dishes are hygienic, and people like to eat off them. Yet, they do take time to wash, and they will get dirty again. There are a lot of things like that in life. How you interpret them is up to you.

 ————————————————————————

Intentionally Making Meaning

We should not think of our past as definitely settled. . . . My past changes every minute according to the meaning given it now, in this moment.

CZESLAW MILOSZ

"The question is," said Alice, "whether you can make words mean so many different things."

"The question is," said Humpty Dumpty, "which is to be master—that's all."

LEWIS CARROLL

Meaning is the experience of seeing one thing in relation to another. The common reactive myth says that events and objects have true, intended meanings based on true stories that link them to other events and objects. According to that myth, the meanings are there waiting to be discovered, most likely the obvious ones given by your parents, friends, and the media. You have no choice.

On my livingroom mantel stands a vase that my daughter Karen made when she was young. I can see it as just a vase. Or I can enrich its meaning by letting it stand for Karen and her energy and creativity. If I should break it, I could dramatize the event and turn it into tragedy by recalling her making it and seeing its loss as symbolic of her growing up and leaving home. Or I could accept that I have no vase and lots of pottery bits. I could use its loss to spur me to treasure Karen whenever I am with her, because I will not always be.

Meaning exists only in the experience of living beings. Different people find different meanings in the *same* event because they relate the event to other objects and events differently. You can deliberately choose your stories to give life a loving meaning. You can, like Humpty Dumpty, be master over your meanings.

Practice 23

CHANGE THE MEANING BY CHANGING THE STORY

Where do we come from? Where are we going? What is the meaning of this life? That is what every heart is shouting, what every head is asking as it beats on chaos.

NIKOS KAZANTZAKIS

This is the first of several practices in which you intentionally create various meanings for the *same* events. This keeps you from being trapped by stories you learned long ago. It frees you to create experiences the way you choose to.

Recall an event in your life that did not turn out the way you wanted it. Head a page in your journal with the bare facts of the event. Think back to the actual event and write a paragraph or two of the story, interpreting it negatively. Dramatize the loss, pain, or embarrassment, as if you were writing a melodrama.

Next write a paragraph or two of story, interpreting the event positively. Emphasize how it helped the people involved to grow, freed them to move on and live out different paths that were more suited to them. Describe how the event strengthened, or could strengthen, those who experienced it, how those people could use it to have more insight and compassion, to be more loving.

Can you pour yourself into either story, as you choose? How does your experience of the event shift as you dramatize one story or the other? Willful reinterpretation of events is a powerful tool for eliminating heartfelt nos and replacing them with maybes and yeses.

As another example, if you and your spouse decide to separate, that might mean your marriage was a failure, you should never have gotten together, and one or both of you are terrible people. It also might mean you have helped each other to learn and love, and in the process have grown apart so that now is the time to go off on your own, grateful for the experiences, ready to learn and love with other people in other ways. With that interpretation, you can love this person who has been such an important part of your life, forever.

 ——————————————————————

And life is what we make it, always has been, always will be.
GRANDMA MOSES

4 ❦ OPENING YOUR HEART TO THE WORLD

Till the very end of time
matter will always remain young,
exuberant
sparkling
newborn
for those who are willing.
TEILHARD DE CHARDIN

Cultivating Your Approach to Events

I am sitting on the sofa in the family room next to Elizabeth, who is ten. We are looking at an overturned wastebasket, kitten toys, backpack, games, playing cards, somebody's lunch bag, scissors, snippets of paper, colored pens and pencils, books, blocks, a marble, and two paper ornaments left over from Christmas three months ago. I say to her, "Just look at the litter in this room! It's shocking, disgraceful." Elizabeth says, "It looks like love to me."

It is all a matter of how you approach the world. With your heart open to see and interpret what you find with a heartfelt yes, you can create constant wonder at the joy of living.

> *"Open your eyes," God shouts: "I want to see!*
> *Prick up your ears, I want to hear!*
> *March in the front ranks: you are my head!"*
> NIKOS KAZANTZAKIS

Practice 24

CREATE YOUR WORLD THROUGH YOUR ATTENTION

When you realize that you are the light of the world, you will also realize that you are the love of it; that to know is to love and to love is to know.

SRI NISARGADATTA MAHARAJ

Whoever you are: some evening take a step
 out of your house, which you know so well.
Enormous space is near, your house lies where it begins,
 whoever you are.
Your eyes find it hard to tear themselves
 from the sloping threshold, but with your eyes
Slowly, slowly, lift one black tree
 up so it stands against the sky, skinny, alone.
With that you have made the world.

RAINER MARIA RILKE

As "the light of the world," you are like a flashlight with a colored lens, probing through the dark in a vast world of unlimited richness. You see only what you point the flashlight at, and only in the color of the lens you are using. Thus you project onto the world your own attitude or spirit.

As you project love, you experience love. There are several aspects to how you approach an event.

- what you *believe* about yourself and it
- what you *intend* as you approach it
- your habits of *attention* that filter its many features
- your *interpretations and judgments* of it
- what it *means* to you

In this book we treat each of these aspects of your approach to events so that you can choose them intentionally to become more loving.

You are able to focus your sensing sharply onto particular features of the world that are important to you. If you are hungry, all your senses scan for food; if you are scared, all your senses scan for the threat. This is a practice in precisely this kind of selective sensing. Through it you will become more and more sensitive. Sensitivity means awareness, acute awareness. The more sensitive you are, the more you note and appreciate even small details, and your heightened awareness of the world makes your actions more effective.

This practice is an attention game that you can play anytime and anyplace regardless of circumstances. Close your eyes and clear your mind for a minute. Then open your eyes and, with full determination, scan everything in sight for straight lines. Notice one straight line after another. There may be few of them or hundreds. As soon as you see a straight line, leave it and look for another. Spend no time on anything else. When you have exhausted the straight lines visible to you, close your eyes and rest.

The next time you open your eyes, scan for the color red. Notice every spot of red around, jumping quickly from one to the next. Hold your attention strongly on looking for red, so nothing distracts you. When you have done red, rest your eyes again. The next time, look for sparkles.

You can play the game with sounds too. Depending on where you are, listen for bird calls, insect sounds, traffic noise, or people talking.

If you are in a public place, scan for happy or sad faces, for people with black or yellow or red hair, for children or teenagers or the elderly, for people who look tired, for loving couples.

Feel the chair or floor or bed under you, pushing up on you and supporting you. Scan your entire body for itches. Feel the air coming in through your nose and filling your lungs, then feel it go out as your lungs contract. With your eyes closed, go over the surface of your body, feeling how your clothing is caressing and warming you.

Attend to the little wrinkles in the face of the person

you are talking to. Notice the highlights in his hair. Listen to the rises and falls in the pitch of his voice, to the rhythm in his words.

If you are touching someone's hair or cheek, for a minute put your whole attention onto just feeling that hair or cheek. If you are kissing someone, simply feel her lips with yours.

Over time, experiment with directing your attention in countless ways, exploring the world in which you live, learning that it has far more to offer than you will ever be able to experience. Notice, as you place your attention in one place, how the rest of the world disappears, how you create your world through selective attention. On your path of loving, employ this ability selectively to love, rather than to have some of the other experiences possible in your circumstances.

It is important to draw the distinction between sensitivity, which Practice 24 sharpens, and vulnerability. *Sensitivity* means heightened awareness, while *vulnerability* means putting your experience into the hands of events. In particular, vulnerability means adding your own upset to pain or threat of pain, either your own or another's. Vulnerability is the opposite of loving: it puts responsibility for your own heartfelt no onto the nos of the rest of the world.

Practice 25

SENSING AS LOVING

There isn't any secret formula or method. You learn by loving— by paying attention and doing what you thereby discover has to be done.

ALDOUS HUXLEY

For thirty years I (studied Zen under a Master.)
How many times the leaves fell, the buds came out!

But after I really saw the peach blossoms,
Not another doubt did I have!

REIUN

I am sitting in the living room reading, when Karen, who is fourteen, enters. She draws for a few minutes while I read. I look up and *will* as hard as I can to love her—to appreciate her spirit, warmth, beauty, and aliveness. I surrender to her. She seems not to notice me, puts down her pen, and goes out of the room. As she reaches the landing, she suddenly says, "Oh, I feel just wonderful!" She puts her arms up and twirls across the dining room, then dances out into the kitchen, graceful and happy. Warmed, I go back to reading. Somehow, I have just taken part in a miracle.

Your experience of relation to the world—whether you are one with it, part of it, or alien to it—depends on what you believe to be the case. Your relatedness to the world is another self-confirming myth. Of course, you cannot change your reality just by mouthing something like, "I love the world and the world loves me." But you can practice the orientation of mutual loving, and over time you will hold the world in love and grow to know you are held in love by it.

In this practice, you radiate love to each object that you sense. With your eyes you beam loving energy onto whatever you see. With your hands you caress whatever you touch. As you listen to the robin, you bless it with all your heart as it hops about on your lawn. How much loving energy can you muster to send forth with your senses?

Practice 26

SENSING AS BEING LOVED

Faith is the opening of all sides and every level of one's life to the divine inflow.

MARTIN LUTHER KING, JR.

You say Thou to (the tree) and give yourself to it, and it says
Thou to you and gives itself to you. . . . Something lights up and
approaches us from the source of being.

MARTIN BUBER

This is the complement of Practice 25. Rather than radiating love, you use your senses to receive the world's love for you. If you do not interpret the world as loving you, you will never feel loved. To be loved means to be the recipient of another's heartfelt yes. This can be the yes of the sun as it warms your body. This can be the yes of your food as it delights and nourishes you, of the bird singing from the telephone wire, or of the mail carrier who brings the morning's junk mail.

Imagine that the world has deliberately set up the circumstances around you so that everything you see, hear, taste, and feel has been beamed toward you as expressions of a deeply felt yes directed at you. Instead of being someone looking at a cloud, know that what you see is the cloud sending its yes to you. Instead of petting your cat, feel that cat as offering to comfort your hand in the deepest love. The water loves you by quenching your thirst. The music caresses your ears.

In your initial attempts at this kind of sensing, you may not prove very skillful. Even the world's greatest ice skaters were not very skillful when they put on their first pair of metal blades and wobbled out onto the ice. A life of love is not the work of a single afternoon.

 ───────────────────────────────────

Mindfulness—Developing a Powerful Aim

If we are to set a Purpose, it is this: to transubstantiate matter and
turn it into spirit.

NIKOS KAZANTZAKIS

Where you go, employ all your heart.
THE SHU KING

In every moment of your waking life, you are aimed. Your *aim* is what you have your attention on right now. You could think of it as the answer to the question, "Where am I?" Maybe it is reading this sentence, wiggling around in the chair to become more comfortable, coming up with the right words to express what you want to say, or rubbing your itchy eye.

In most of your moments, you probably have little sense that you *willed* the direction your attention is aimed. You may have willed your *goal*—a concrete destination such as to wash the dishes or to read this book—but not your momentary aim as you wander toward that goal. But you *could* will that aim. You could aim to love, at any moment and whatever you may be doing.

If you want to go in any particular direction, you have to put together some moments in which you are pointed that way. The more moments you are pointed east, the farther east you will get. This overall direction of movement, whether willfully chosen or determined by circumstances, is your *purpose*. It differs from a goal in that goals are concrete. You know whether you have reached a goal —either the dishes are clean or they are not. Purpose is the answer to the question, "What am I here for?" The answer might be, "Just to get the dishes washed." But if you want to love while you wash, the answer might be, "To delight in every moment as I wash these dishes."

Even if your purpose is to get the dishes washed, your momentary aim cannot be to wash the dishes. Washing the dishes is not the act of a moment, it is the act of twenty minutes. You *can* aim to rub the grease off this pan; rubbing off this grease is a momentary act. You can align your aim with your purpose by picking up and washing this dish, then that dish, until they are all clean. Or you can let your aim wander all over the place while you take longer getting the dishes washed.

There is an inescapable fact about being human: *You* have to decide what the purpose of your life is. And by living from that decision, you will go in that direction. That is, you give your life the purpose you choose.

Throughout human history, most people had little purpose beyond survival and doing what their ancestors did. Compared to them, we are incredibly free. We can assert a purpose for life, even though we realize it may be only tentative, in order to have a direction within which life takes on perspective. For a loving life, choose loving as a major life purpose.

When you ask, "What am I here for?" in order to determine your purpose, do not look to circumstances to give you the answer. *State* your purpose—to love—and let that, rather than how you feel or what you want in the moment, decide the matter.

Loving is an apt choice for the purpose of a life that would otherwise be an endless cycle of chasing—you go after this, which is useful for that, which is useful for something else, which is useful for still something else. Where does this cycle end? A sleeping bag and a good-fitting pair of boots are useful for an overnight hike, but that hike is just one more thing to live through, unless you can turn it into joy. While your loving may affect the world in a myriad of positive ways, choose loving as your purpose for the sake of the experience, which is an end in itself.

 ——————————————————————

Practice 27

LEARNING MINDFULNESS

If the heart wanders or is distracted, bring it back to the point quite gently and replace it tenderly in its Master's presence. And even if you did nothing during the whole of your hour but bring your heart back and place it again in Our Lord's presence, though it went away every time you brought it back, your hour would be very well employed.

ST. FRANCIS OF SALES

Mindfulness is the practice of aiming your attention, moment by moment, in the direction of your purpose. It is called mindfulness because you have to keep your purpose in mind as you watch your attention. Then whenever you notice that your aim has drifted off purpose, you calmly realign it.

The practice of mindfulness, in one of its many forms, has played an important role in the lives of countless people throughout recorded history. They have based their spiritual lives on it and have used it to accomplish endless tasks, especially the most difficult. To cultivate a powerful aim:

1. Know your purpose—the answer to the question, "What am I here for?"
2. Notice your aim—the answer to the question, "Where am I?" Where is your attention focused right now?
3. Keep your aim aligned with your purpose. When it wanders away, simply place your attention back in the direction of your intention, without distracting yourself further by telling yourself how dumb you are for being distracted.

If you have ever practiced meditation, you have practiced this pattern. Your purpose might have been to sit quietly attending to your breath. Each time you noticed that your attention had wandered off, you simply brought it back to your breath.

Again, when you have been successful at concentrating, you also have practiced this pattern. You had a purpose, which might have been to write a letter, play some music, or win a game. As soon as you observed your attention aimed elsewhere, toward a distraction, you brought it calmly back to the letter, music, or game.

You can practice mindfulness at any time. For example, as you read this book, ask what your purpose is every once in a while. Your answer might be, "to create in my mind the meaning of these words so I can learn to love more often and more richly and enjoy myself in the process." But you might also find that your aim is to find fault, pass judgment, agree or disagree with what is written. Are you playing the role of editor or critic, or the person who wants to get the most possible out of the book?

Whenever you decide to do a practice in this book, you accept it as your purpose. Then notice your momentary aim by looking at what you are focused on, right now. Do not try to figure out your aim from your purpose. Your purpose could be to love, while your aim might be to shout profanity at someone crowding in front of you at a traffic light. You cannot figure out your aim. You can notice it, and intentionally place it.

Mindfulness means choosing what you are looking for so that what you find will be what you want. If you want to make your life more loving, pre-choose the answer to the question, "What am I here for?" Let that answer be, "To love!" Then practice mindfulness with that purpose.

Practice 28

DRIVING AS MINDFULNESS PRACTICE

You never really learn to swear until you learn to drive.
ANONYMOUS (QUOTED BY ARTHUR BLOCH)

The persons in the street get in my way because I collide with them as possible rivals. I shall like them as soon as I see them as partners in the struggle.

TEILHARD DE CHARDIN

Driving is a common activity that offers a never-ending supply of unexpected challenges to hold to a loving purpose. In particular, unfairness on the road seems to be rewarded over and over, as those who take chances and do not play by the rules push ahead of those who play it safe. Driving is therefore a perfect time to practice mindfulness. In order to drive a car (or bicycle) lovingly, you have to direct compassion toward a stream of other seemingly immoral and inept drivers and, just as often, toward yourself, when you notice the grip that your habits of negative judgment have on you. As you drive

1. Hold the purpose of loving it all—of delighting in the journey with compassion and relaxed acceptance of other drivers, regardless of what they do. Instead of driving just to get to work or some other destination, be happily in the moment with the trucks, cars, sky, houses, and road.
2. Let your goal be to reach your destination safely and legally.
3. See yourself engaged in a complex enterprise in which everyone is cooperating for the common good.
4. Notice yourself with compassion when you divert from your purpose and react with frustration or anger. When you find yourself sucked away by events, calmly give up your anger or win/lose attitude and bring your attention back to loving.

Know in advance that you will experience the entire range of driving skill and courtesy on the road. There is no way you can get only the best part of that range for yourself—all of it will show up. Notice that you, like everyone else, sometimes drive more safely and more courteously than at other times, and thus present your own range of courtesy and skill to the other drivers on the road.

From one viewpoint on the road, people are speeding, tailgating, lane-hopping, cutting one another off, committing to dangerous courses of action, and then brazening it out in order to prove themselves right.

There are jackrabbit starts, screeching stops, anger, shouts, gestures, and failure to admit mistakes. From the viewpoint of a helicopter flying overhead, taxis, cars, trucks, and buses fill the streets and move in such a coordinated and cooperative way that everyone seems to sense what everyone else wants to do, and all join together so that everyone can do it. Whether driving is cooperation or competition depends how you approach it.

When you reach your destination, take a moment to congratulate yourself on getting there safely with a loving purpose. Through this practice of mindfulness you will increasingly view humans—yourself and others—with deep compassion. You will be able to live in love in the presence of a much wider range of circumstances than you might now think possible.

Practice 29

ATTENTION AS CARING

You can give your whole attention only when you care, which means that you really love.

J. KRISHNAMURTI

This practice is an exercise in *caring* for whatever it is that you are attending to. In one sense it is obvious that whatever you are attending to is what you care most about right now. After all, you are attending to this, rather than anything else you could be doing, so it must be the most important for the moment.

But *caring* is different from *attention*. Machines can attend, but they do not care. Caring-driven attention emphasizes interest and concern for the well-being of what you are attending to. Since you are going to attend to one thing after another for the rest of your life, you are going to care for one thing after another. In this practice you *really* care, enormously, for what you would otherwise approach as just another everyday event.

On the left side of a sheet of paper, write the heading What Matters to Me? On the right side write What Does Not Matter to Me? As you reflect on these headings, list people, tasks, places, objects, ideas, all kinds of items that come to mind.

For those items in the right column, ask yourself why you choose to do something that you do not care about. What motives got you to put your attention onto this person, this object, this task, this idea? Be aware of the caring for your own life and perhaps the lives of others that is in the background when you choose, for example, to do the laundry. Can you move the laundry from the right-hand to the left-hand list, and handle the laundry as a deep expression of caring for yourself and these others?

Head a page with What Will I Commit to Seeing as If It Mattered? Under it list items from the right-hand list that you are willing to work at. Then, when you confront one of these items in your daily life, pour yourself into seeing it as important and worthwhile.

Wherever you have your attention placed right now, beyond any reasons you might list for placing it there, know you have chosen to attend to this because you care about it. Since that is so, see how strongly you can really care. Pour out your love, let your life in this moment be a caress of whatever objects you are involved with, and through them caress other people, yourself, and the world. Fill whatever action you are engaged in with caring.

This practice shows you where you are "just going through the motions," or are doing things because you think you have to. It shows you areas of living that are ripe for transformation as you follow a path of loving.

You can learn to make anything matter to you. Just approach it as if it matters, treat it as if it matters, pay total attention to it, and your experience will confirm its importance to you. This approach is the essence of intentional loving. You willfully choose to see this (of all things!) as if it mattered so much that you are overwhelmed with caring for it, with loving it. As you go through your daily life, your attention is always focused, shifting from one person, animal, object, task, activity, or thought to another. That item always poses to you the question, Am I willing to see this as mattering deeply to me? Am I willing to love this?

❧ ———————————————————————————— ❧

Practice 30

ALL-OUT APPRECIATION

Oh, earth, you're too wonderful for anybody to realize you.
THORNTON WILDER

The heavens declare the glory of God;
and the firmament sheweth his handiwork.
OLD TESTAMENT, PSALM 19

When you look back over a lifetime on the path of love, it will be clear to you that the whole path was just this one practice. All the other practices and ideas and inspirations served as aids to strengthen you in this lifetime practice.

This is the practice of intentional loving. You devote a period of time solely to appreciating whatever is before you. You value it, enjoy it, esteem it. You approach it from a powerful yes, determined to use all the sensitivity you are capable of to experience it through that interpretation. You practice mindfulness, keeping in mind that your purpose here is to appreciate, and sensitivity, as you learn to appreciate nuances that you might never have even noticed before.

To begin, set the timer for five minutes. Sit before a single flower and set your purpose to be simply to appreciate it. Let that purpose spur you to a creative positive interaction with the flower. How strongly can you appreciate the flower in those five minutes?

As you practice, choose different time intervals and different objects to appreciate. Employ what you have learned from all the other sensitivity and loving practices you have done. Slow down your senses, as you would to look at a famous painting, and revel in what is before you. Open to this object. Does your skin or body feel like a boundary or wall between the object and you? Can you make your skin, with its sense organs, into an opening to the object, and through it an opening to the entire universe?

In order to do these practices, you have to be willing to give over to something else, even with all its faults, the power to move you. If you do this, it may seem as if you were deceived by it. You might, for example, find out that your friends dislike someone you love, or you might find later that you dislike the person yourself.

But that is not the point of loving. Loving is not a judgment you pass on the qualities of something, either now or once and for all. Loving is a way you choose to experience something, right now. You can marvel at the beauty and skill of a rattlesnake even as you evade its strike, even as you may feel obliged to kill it. This issue of judgment and its role in loving is so important that we devote the next chapter to it.

O world, I cannot hold thee close enough!
EDNA ST. VINCENT MILLAY

5 ❦ JUDGMENTS
AND DEMANDS

By saying that it is good or bad we put an end to thinking. . . . It is love that destroys the sense of the inferior and the superior.

J. KRISHNAMURTI

Making Judgments

Judge not, that you be not judged. For with the judgment you pronounce you will be judged, and the measure you give will be the measure you get.

JESUS

There is a widespread belief that loving is a judgment you make on the merits of what you love. The cost of this belief is enormous. Whenever you approach the world as a judge, you will evaluate some of what you see as good and some as bad, and the rest as average. That is the inevitable result of judgment.

For example, when you are at a party, the people there will vary in how much they attract your romantic interest. Approach them as a judge and you set up standards. By refusing to appreciate anyone who does not measure up, you will not enjoy anyone who is not a potential romantic partner. In effect, you have made a *demand* that must be met before you are willing to love someone. Whatever your demand, it has not changed any of the people at the party —they are all still there. You have simply decided not to appreciate the ones you deem unlovable.

As a judge, you live your life under the threat of judgment—your own and that of others. However you fare in these countless judgments, they menace you. Even when others do not care a bit, you will be caught up in "How am I doing? Do I measure up? Am I good enough?" As you judge others, you will be judged. This is hardly the way to live life as a heartfelt yes.

So before you go to the party, ask yourself what your purpose is in attending. Is it the same as a teacher grading exams? That is, are you there to grade people, to judge them on some feature, like their attractiveness? Or are you at the party to delight in the experience? If so, give up judging them and appreciate as many as you can. What really makes something lovable is not the fact that it excels other objects in quality, but the fact that it exists and is in your life.

❧ ─────────────────────────────── ❧

Practice 31

WHAT IS THE ROLE OF JUDGMENT IN YOUR LIFE?

The more you learn about how judgment stifles your loving, the better you will be able to take the power out of your judgments. Certainly, a voice in your mind will continue to judge and evaluate, but you will not have to take it so seriously. In fact, you will often hear that voice as unnecessary, indeed as grandiose, because it implies that the way it says the world should be is the way the world *really should* be. You will see your love or rejection of something as your own personal response to it, rather than your discovery of its true merits, and the rest of the world will not seem so wrong for not agreeing with you. This practice will give you power to use judgment in ways that do not interfere with loving, and to refuse to judge at all when judging does not serve you.

Make a list in your journal of the people, events, places, activities, and anything else that comes to mind that you frequently judge. You make these judgments in conversations, in writing, and internally in your mind. By each one, note down your typical judgment.

For example, "I judge shopping as fun but cooking and dishwashing as necessary evils." "At work I judge Paul as an obnoxious jerk but Bill as warm and supportive."

Next, consider how these judgments affect your love for each item on your list. What is your experience of the item when you are passing judgment? How might you experience cooking if you stopped judging it as drudgery and paid attention to it instead? Experiment with giving up judgment for various periods of time and paying close attention to the item. For instance, simply work with Paul without evaluating what he says or does. How hard or easy is it? In what way does your experience change? In the absence of the judging voice, is the reality of dishwashing different from the reality of most other activities?

Head a page in your journal Who and What Is It My Job to Judge? Then list what comes to mind, including the items from the first part of this practice, and note beside each one what justifies you in judging this item. For those entries where your judging seems justified, in what sense is that so? For example, you certainly choose what to do and what not to do, moment by moment, by judging which actions are best for you. Also, you judge your children's actions to assure their safety.

Every time you judge, you assume that it is your business to judge, that one of the purposes of your life is to pass judgment on what you find. You may conclude that you have done enough of that, that you do not need to make it part of your job every day to evaluate other people.

 ———————————————————————

Making Comparisons

To set up what you like against what you dislike—this is the disease of the mind.

SENG TSAN, THIRD PATRIARCH OF ZEN

Comparison is a form of judging. To compare, you focus not on this object, but on similar ones from the past that you think were better or worse than this. But regardless of your comparisons, every person, spider, blade of grass, grain of sand, or molecule is lovable, and there are people who can and do love them. It takes the same habit and skill to delight in the turtledove singing from the telephone line as to delight in my little girl, who brought the tire pump into the bedroom "to leave it where it belongs." In both cases, the delight is delight. Comparison kills love.

Charles Schulz's Charlie Brown said, "Life is like an ice cream cone: You have to learn to lick it." When you lick a strawberry ice cream cone, your entire attention could be, like that of a child, on the cold, sweet, smooth flavor. Or it could be on how you have always liked chocolate better than strawberry, and how this ice cream has more air blown into it than some other brand. You are stuck in the universal human predicament: It is strawberry, not chocolate, and it is full of air, and it is melting. You will either eat it with joy, eat it grudgingly, or let it melt.

You live in a sea of comparisons. Rankings of athletes and sporting teams fill the newspapers. We find the *best-looking* people from beauty contests and the *smartest* from IQ tests. We rank orchestra members by their chair, businesses by their profit, nations by their GNP, and everyone by their salary.

Growing up in this sea of comparisons makes it easy to get in the habit of comparing yourself—your body and performance—with other people's, and thereby not appreciating your own life because it does not measure up. You can find endless standards for comparing, and you can always raise your standards. You can look for the best and then the best of the best, until you have reason to find fault with everyone and everything. Oh, you may make room for one lonely soul on top of the heap, one lovely spot as the most beautiful, one dream job that could fulfill your desires.

What is before you now is what you get to love now, however you might compare it with others. Every time you postpone loving until something better comes up, you are saying no to loving whatever is at hand. Loving is always this day, this moment, now—this person, this object, this task. This one is always the right one to love, because it is the one before you.

❧ ———————————————————————————————— ❧

Practice 32

PAY ATTENTION TO COMPARISONS

Love means to stop comparing.
BERNARD GRASSET

In this practice you observe the amount of comparison that goes on within and around you and see how common it is. You just watch it, witness it, without taking a stand about whether any particular act of comparison is appropriate or valuable. In time, this practice will free you from comparing automatically and thereby limiting your loving. Yet you will still be able to use comparisons whenever you choose.

Pay attention to comparisons you find in the media, expressed in conversations by others and by yourself, and in your own mind as you talk to yourself throughout the day. Scan through your newspaper or newsmagazine and mark every place something or someone is compared or ranked. Become aware of the sea of comparisons that you live in, of how often you are urged to compare your home with that of a professional decorator, your country or community with others, your food with that of a gourmet cook, your job with that of the most *successful* people, your body with that of a model.

When you hear the voice inside your mind comparing or judging, note the words in your journal. You will acquire a list of judgments and comparisons pronounced by your internal voice on the world and on yourself.

Do the same with preferences. Notice how important you and others think it is to express a preference, how world-shaking it seems to decide that you prefer this brand of soap to that, or this musician to that one. It seems so much more important than simply enabling you to pick something to buy when you get to the store. How much do you want to convince others that your preferences are universal—that they should agree with you because you are right in your judgment? Yet how much difference do most of these preferences really make?

Note which comparisons are objective: "I have gained seven pounds." "Elizabeth is four inches taller than Karen." Note those that are personal opinions (regardless of how much others may agree with them) for which you take responsibility: "I like Van Gogh better than Rembrandt." Note those that are personal opinions for which you deny responsibility by claiming they are objective: "Van Gogh was a better painter than Rembrandt." Note any personal comparisons you make as sweeping claims about the inherent nature of things: "I am stupid." "He's just a genius at mathematics."

By observing the sea of comparisons and judgments in which you live, you will see them as simply relative rankings that people make up. Sometimes it may be useful to make them, but you need not take them so seriously and let them determine who or what you will love. Comparing is not loving; it just gets in the way.

Rather than deaden life with judgments of *better* and *worse*, you can interpret differences simply as differences and revel in variety. You can do this even when it seems obvious that your likes and dislike stem from objects that really are better or worse, good or bad. Differences offer handles on which to hang your love. Surrender to the uniqueness of whatever is before you and delight in the features it has to offer, looking at it through your memories of similar objects from the past only when it serves your purpose to love.

Practice 33

APPRECIATE SOMETHING YOU TAKE
FOR GRANTED

The world will never starve for want of wonders; but only for want of wonder.

G. K. CHESTERTON

In music, in the sea, in a flower, in a leaf, in an act of kindness . . . I see what people call God in all these things.

PABLO CASALS

I will be the gladdest thing under the sun!
I will touch a hundred flowers and not pick one.

EDNA ST. VINCENT MILLAY

In this practice you intentionally love a person, object, or activity that you take for granted—something you feel sure you already know well, that holds no interest or importance for you, that you have put out of your mind. It may be something you value in only one way, like a person who is there only to type your letters. It may be someplace where you have been before and "already know what it's like."

The challenge is to experience thoroughly and to appreciate what is there before you, with whatever qualities it has. The less obviously interesting the object, the more creative you will have to be in finding something to appreciate, thus the more you will learn from doing this practice.

Find an object in your immediate vicinity that you take for granted. Turn your attention toward it and, for a period of time, commit yourself to appreciating it wholeheartedly in every way you can find. Look at it from different angles, study the play of lights and darks, enjoy its design or form as it contrasts with its background, reflect on its utility, its history, on the components that make it up, where they came from, and who was involved in getting them here.

Do the same with an activity or job that you believe

is just something to finish. Do you find yourself holding back because it does not seem right to engage fully in this object or activity with enthusiasm and joy?

If you make this a regular practice, you will stop taking things in your life for granted and instead make them parts of the extraordinary world that includes you as well. The word *ordinary* is a curse you put on something to relegate it to the discard pile, where you can ignore it forever. This is worse than other curses, because when people hear it, they nod their heads in agreement rather than tell you that you are off the mark. *Ordinary* says something about the one who speaks it, and nothing about the object.

Here is a sample meditation on something that is easy to take for granted.

❧ ———————————————————————— ❧

Appreciating a Cup of Tea

It is very deep to have a cup of tea.
KATAGIRI ROSHI

A wise man tastes the entire Tigris in every sip.
GHALIB (MIRZA ASADULLAH BEG KHAN)

Deep brown, tending just a bit toward red beneath the surface. Wisps of steam rising and I can feel them heat my face. Three little bubbles clustered together on one edge, not quite caught up in the surface swirl. What looks like a small oil slick on the surface, and the sparkling reflections of the lights overhead.

The familiar smell that I associate with those years in England when I kept warm by drinking tea, and with decades of mornings when I started off my day this way. It reminds me of Jane, who introduced me to this brand of tea on that magical evening so long ago. And of Mother, who made tea for me when I was sick with the measles when I was nine or ten, and who carefully held the cup to my mouth so I wouldn't spill it. This tea links me with countless loving moments from my past.

This tea started as buds growing on bushes on an island in the Indian Ocean, and it was tended and harvested and dried by workers there, whose images I can picture and whose culture and language are rich and fascinating. It was shipped by truck to port, packed into a ship, and sailed across the Pacific to Los Angeles. There it was shipped by truck to a factory where it was blended, put in bags, and boxed. Three more times it was shipped by truck until it reached the grocery where I bought it. This tea links me directly with hundreds of people, and indirectly with all of life.

The water in this cup has been around ever since the earth formed some four and a half billion years ago. Over and over, countless times, that water has cycled—evaporating into the air, forming into clouds, raining or snowing, filling lakes, rivers, streams, and snowfields, incorporated into the bodies of plants and animals, and always returning to the oceans. In this very cup are some 200,000 water molecules that were in the body, at any particular moment, of any single human adult who has ever lived. Trillions of these molecules I am drinking have resided in each person's body at some time in his life. Some of this water that is entering my body has been in the bodies of every plant, every animal, every human who has ever lived. This tea links me physically with all life.

The energy that heated this tea came through metal wires hooked to a power plant that burns oil, which was taken from beneath the sands of a country on the other side of the globe, loaded into a tanker, and shipped to California. The energy stored in that oil came to earth originally as sunlight, was trapped millions of years ago in microscopic plants and animals, and was finally buried under what is now Saudi Arabia, where it was preserved to warm my morning cup of tea so many years later. I warm my hands with that heat.

As I drink the tea, I perform a ritual of humanity dating back over a million years to the time people tamed fire, thereby linking myself with all men and women who have warmed themselves with a hot drink. Now let me taste it.

Conditional Loving

We always affirm with conditions. I affirm the world on condition that it gets to be the way Santa Claus told me it ought to be. But affirming it the way it is—that's the hard thing.

JOSEPH CAMPBELL

> *Perfect like great space,*
> *The way has nothing lacking,*
> *nothing in excess.*
> SENG TSAN, THIRD PATRIARCH OF ZEN

Out of habit you search everything for flaws, and of course you find them. But because you want to love, and this object *is* worthy, and you do not want to give up on it, you stick a few conditions on your love: "I will love you if you get a better job." Now, by that you might mean you will continue spending time with her if she gets a better job, but you also might mean that you will stifle any delight for her until she has a job with more pay and responsibility.

If so, you are postponing loving by a bribe. Unconditional loving does not depend on the future—it means responding to this, right here, right now, just as it is. It frees your beloved to grow, rather than bribing her by withholding your love until she grows in the direction you want.

Conditional loving is, at best, postponed loving. Every minute you postpone loving means one less minute of love-time in this lifetime. You can keep waiting and waiting for "the right one" to come along, and it never does. Or by the time it does, you have imposed some other condition. *This isn't it* and *this is it* are self-confirming approaches to whatever is before you. If you are waiting for life to *make* you react with love, know that *this* is life. This! It is this one or no one, now or never.

Loving cannot be a mistake, whatever the future might bring. Suppose you stand in awe before a painting and someone tells you it was made by a kid in nursery school. You then have the choice of feeling either stupid or proud for having been so moved by the work of a child. Fear a mistake and you will hold off loving anything until your judgment is ratified by the future or by a panel of experts.

Loving is not inspecting hams, stamping purple seals on them, scared to death that someone will find out you stamped grade A on a ham that is really grade B. If you confuse grading hams with loving them, you will close your heart out of fear of being conned.

This is not to gloss over flaws or make believe they do not exist. It is just that you do not have to go to extremes the moment you notice the flaw: "I wanted to love this— I was all set to love this. But now it fails by this crucial standard to live up to what it should be—to what everyone knows it should be." The flaw is obviously there, so you cannot deny it, and you will not get past it.

Everything that you ever receive will come to you in a flawed vessel. All vessels are flawed. That one swears too much, that one makes too little money, that one has a mole on his cheek, and that one laughs too loud. Every blessing, every lesson, comes in a flawed vessel. You can focus either on the contents of the vessel or on the flaw. If you do not like the role someone plays in your life, you will see a flaw in him. If you focus on it, get lost in negative judgment, you have no way either to love him or to learn from him. There he is—glorious, flaw and all—and here you are muttering about what a terrible thing it is that he does what he does. Thus you waste your blessings.

❦ ──────────────────────────────── ❦

Practice 34

WHAT CONDITIONS HAVE YOU PLACED ON LOVING?

There is a crack in everything God has made.
RALPH WALDO EMERSON

The Perfect Way is difficult only for those who pick and choose.
SENG TSAN, THIRD PATRIARCH OF ZEN

This practice will clarify the conditions you have placed on loving. Once you see what they are, you will be free to work to meet some of them and to love despite the fact that others are not met.

List in your notebook some tasks, activities, objects, places, and people with whom your experience is sometimes negative. For each one, write a sentence that starts, "I could love _____ if _____," and finish with whatever conditions come to mind. "I could love the view out of my window if the lawn were mowed and there were no dandelions and I trimmed the willow tree."

Examine each condition to see whether it is in your power to meet it and how hard it would be to meet it. For some of the items, actually do what it takes to meet the conditions and then appreciate the result. Do you really love the result when the conditions are fulfilled, or do you come up with new conditions or hit some other block to loving? Are you *willing* to love this object, or are you using conditions to keep a heartfelt yes at bay?

❦ ──────────────────────────────── ❦

Practice 35

LOVE IT UNCONDITIONALLY

When you look at anything, it is the ultimate you see, but you imagine that you see a cloud or a tree.
SRI NISARGADATTA MAHARAJ

This is the practice of unconditional loving. Pick an item on the list you made in Practice 34. Pretend that you know you *could* love that item, right now, if only you chose to. The conditions you have written merely note flaws in a vessel that contains a blessing. You have paid enough attention to those flaws.

Visualize yourself, the next time you approach this item, determined to look beyond its flaws, to value and enjoy its other features. Carry the visualization through to a satisfactory end. Visualization is a useful way of rehearsing an activity in advance that otherwise might be dominated by your old habits.

Then, when you next confront the item, love it despite its flaws. It contains a gift—the opportunity for you to love it and to learn to love in the process. It is just one challenge for loving out of an endless number of such challenges. Each has its own features, so the particulars of your love will differ with each. You have been taught that you love because you find the features good enough, but the cause of love is always the loving way you approach the object.

Schedule *acceptance breaks* during the day in which you notice what features of life are not meeting your conditions for loving, and you deliberately accept, rather than resist, them. In time, change these to *loving breaks* in which you determine to love whatever is in your life at the moment.

 ———————————————————————————————

Having Expectations

Most of us go through life not knowing what we want, but feeling darned sure this isn't it.

ANONYMOUS

It is easy to interpret what you want as something you must have. When you demand that something live up to your standard of judgment before you will love it, you live in your pictures rather than in what is. Since what is always falls short of your pictures, you focus solely on the difference.

You can delight in someone or demand that someone conform to your pictures, but not both. By holding on to your pictures you will feel you are right, and people may agree about how right you are. That way you may be able to manipulate people, change them, fight them, gossip about them, make them wrong, and create all kinds of melodramas involving them. But you will not be able to love them, because there is nothing left but the gap between what you demand and how they show up.

As soon as you demand something, you lose it. If you expect to get $1,000 and get $1,000, you feel you have gotten only what was due. If you get $1,050, you have gotten only $50 more than was due, and if you get $950, you feel cheated out of $50. But if you expect nothing and get $1,000, you can rejoice in every penny!

Live in a world of expectations and you will live in a world of disappointments. Pained by continual disappointments, you will turn to pessimism in an effort to protect yourself from future pain. In this way you will shut out activities that you could delight in and the people who could keep you company.

Everyone is lovable, yet no one has a claim on being loved. Love is a gift from the universe that is offered by individuals. Be grateful that you can play your part in pouring loving energy into the people and objects around you. There can be no higher calling.

Practice 36

WRITE OUT YOUR DEMANDS AND GIVE THEM UP

Write out all of your addictive demands—and see them as a whole. . . . Your mind will not uplevel an addiction to a preference if you don't honestly want to let go of the addiction. You can't fool your mind. You've got to really want to let go—not just want to want to let go.

KEN KEYES, JR.

In this practice you work to take away the power of expectations in affecting your loving. Pick a person or pet or any actual or possible love object. Write out all of your expectations regarding the object, both the ones that it meets and the ones that it does not. Then visualize it as just having failed to meet one or more of your demands and feel your anger, your blaming, your heartfelt no. (For example, your cat just killed a bird.) Then, visualize yourself totally caught up in how wonderful and lovable it is, and revel in your powerful yes. Then pick another demand and visualize it falling short on that one. (Now the cat just had an accident on the rug.) Again, get into your negative feelings as strongly as you can. Then move back to appreciation and love. Then back to an unmet demand. (Now he is sharpening his claws on the sofa.) And so forth.

This practice will develop a habit of responding by *choice*, not by the trigger of met or unmet demands. You will always have a moment before you react when you can choose what you will do. One of those choices, regardless of what has happened and the action you take as a result, is to stay open in a *yes* (not to behavior such as scratching the sofa, but to the cat). When your cat (or, perhaps, your child) violates some standard and you ask yourself, "How could I love someone who does that?" know that the answer is always the same: "Easily. I can love him easily if I will simply look at what is lovable."

The Belief in Scarcity

In the faces of men and women I see God,
and in my own face in the glass,

> *I find letters from God dropped in the street,*
>   *and every one is signed by God's name,*
> *And I leave them where they are, for I know that . . .*
>   *Others will punctually come for ever and ever.*
>
>   WALT WHITMAN

When you judge, compare, and promise to love only when your conditions are met, lovable people are bound to be scarce. If you will not appreciate someone unless you find her in the top 5 percent in intelligence, looks, athletics, and charm, you have ruled out almost everyone. If you ever find someone who does meet your standards, she will almost surely be of the wrong religion, or have some habit you cannot stand, or already be spoken for, or not like you. You will go through life looking for someone who meets your standards, someone worthy of your love, and never find her. How frustrating to be born into a world with so few lovable people!

Yet the lovable is not scarce—it is everywhere. Everything you touch is lovable. There is a huge surplus, a thousand wonderful things to do, see, feel, smell, and taste; a million wonderful people to watch, respond to, talk to, do things for, and delight in; ideas to play with, skills to learn, pictures to paint, songs to sing, grass to mow, poems to write, food to cook, and dishes to wash. Each of these is one more invitation to love, out of countless such.

If you come to your friend out of scarcity, he will suspect you chose him because he was the first one who would have you and the only one you thought you could get. If you love him out of abundance, he will know you enjoy him enough to keep choosing to be with him; that you can find no end of people to love, but when you and he are together, you honor him by choosing him. Coming out of surplus, you love in freedom. The result is neither ambivalence nor resentment, but joy.

To see a World in a Grain of Sand
And a Heaven in a Wild Flower,
Hold Infinity in the palm of your hand
And Eternity in an hour.

WILLIAM BLAKE

6 ❦ HABITS THAT BLOCK LOVING

We grow up never questioning whatever is unquestioned by those around us.

MARGARET MEAD

*I*n this chapter we examine some common habits that seem natural—indeed, almost inevitable—yet block loving. You can work to break these habits and thereby live more lovingly. Breaking a habit does not mean giving up the behavior. It means instead that you are free to choose the behavior when it serves your purpose; thus, you, and not your habits, will control your life.

The Habit of Naysaying

One who walks the Way sees not any faults in the world. Seeing others' faults means that one's own faults are strengthened.

HUI NENG, SIXTH PATRIARCH OF ZEN

Don't scold the lover. The "wrong" way he talks is better than a hundred "right" ways of others.

RUMI

It is easy for your momentary aim to get captured by longtime habits of naysaying, easy to mumble, mumble, gripe, and grumble. If you look at anything through a fault-finding filter, you will find a lot of faults. If you complain to everyone who will listen about how bad things are, you will get lots of agreement. Look out on the yard and attend only to the weeds, and the grass, flowers, and even the trees will disappear. But there will be a lot of weeds!

Which will you see, grass or weeds? This choice is always there to be made, and you can never make it once and for all. Are you willing to make *this* person the right one for loving, *this* house the right one for loving, *this* job the right one . . . for now? This does not imply that you prefer your lawn with weeds, or that you will not work to dig them out. It also does not mean that you cannot tell crabgrass from bluegrass. It means simply that the world is the way it is, weeds and all, and how you experience it is up to you. You might as well love it, regardless of whether you decide to dig out the weeds.

The stance of *no* is arms crossed in judgment—and your verdict seems so all-important. Yet naysaying builds a wall around you. *Yes* lets the world in. *No* keeps it out, defends against it. You may feel safer holding other people, objects, and life on the other side of the wall. Your world will be predictable and familiar, but not very loving.

 ————————————————————————

Practice 37

REPEAT YES INTERNALLY

The big question is whether you are going to be able to say a hearty yes to your adventure.

JOSEPH CAMPBELL

Our thinking machine possesses the capacity to be convinced of anything you like, provided it is repeated often enough and with sufficient conviction.

GEORGE GURDJIEFF

In this practice you interrupt your habit of naysaying before it starts by entering upon life saying yes, rather than no, internally. Simply replace the voice in your mind by repeating yes internally. Let your yes lead your heart in engaging, rather than be a meaningless chant. How strongly can you use this internal reminder to evoke your attitude as you approach the world? You will not melt or be taken advantage of by doing this. Your yes means neither agreement, preference, nor accommodation, but a positive opening to your world.

Just for the sake of learning, but not to strengthen a habit, try saying no instead of yes. How does that affect your experience? Does it make you feel more or less powerful, in control or surrendered, right or wrong? Does your experience close down and get smaller? What is the effect on your ego?

❧ ———————————————————————————— ❧

Practice 38

APPRECIATE WHAT YOU DISLIKE

The basic difference between an ordinary man and a warrior is that a warrior takes everything as a challenge, while an ordinary man takes everything as either a blessing or a curse.

DON JUAN (CARLOS CASTANEDA)

This practice will heighten your awareness of elements in life toward which you normally direct a strong no. It will help you prepare, in advance, for the next time you encounter one, so you will be able to appreciate what is there to appreciate, rather than be caught up in your habit of naysaying.

Make a list of people, animals, places, food, music, activities, and other objects that you habitually dislike. Then review the list and ask, regarding each item, what there is about the item that someone could appreciate. Ask whether you are willing to give up your usual faultfinding when you next encounter it, and see how strongly you can appreciate it. Rehearse in advance what your next encounter with the item might be like, and visualize yourself approaching it determined to use all your creativity and ingenuity to respond to it with a yes.

Then, when you do approach the item, you can break free of your old habit and choose the rehearsed positive behavior instead. Accept the challenge of loving the unlovable, and see how rich the experience is and how much you can learn thereby.

Practice 39

TAKE RESPONSIBILITY FOR WHAT YOU HAVE CHOSEN

I have spent my days stringing and unstringing my instrument while the song I came to sing remains unsung.

RABINDRANATH TAGORE

Choice comes in two flavors: You can decide what you want to do, and then go out and find it, or you can notice what you are already doing, and choose that.

TOM JACKSON

Sometimes you will hear an internal voice saying, "I don't want to be here—I don't want to be doing this." This is the poor-me voice of a victim: "Oh, how I wish I were someplace doing something else!" It is part of a heartfelt no.

Yet in truth you must have other voices telling you to be here and to do this, or else you would not be doing it! You live in the town you live in by choice, you have your job by choice, you maintain all your personal relationships by choice. If, for example, you hate your relationship with someone, you can quit it and live with the consequences of that choice, or you can keep it and turn it into a positive experience.

This practice challenges you, when you are complaining to yourself or someone else, to do something about the complaint, or else to quit complaining and start appreciating. It consists of saying, thinking, or reading the following, while letting its truth sink in deeply.

Given me as I experience me and the world as I perceive it,
of all the places in the world I could be,
of all the things I could be doing,
I have chosen to be here and to be doing this.

This statement must be true, always, every moment. It does not deny that circumstances can limit your freedom. Of course, you sometimes choose to go to work because you want to earn a living or to the dentist to keep your teeth healthy. But it shifts your attention from those limitations to your own array of choices within them.

Practice 40

CARRY LOVE IN YOUR BODY

Smile at each other; smile at your wife, smile at your husband, smile at your children, smile at each other—it doesn't matter who it is—and that will help you to grow up in greater love for each other.

MOTHER TERESA

"How are you?" "Fine." "Well, why don't you tell your face?"

LEO BUSCAGLIA

You can learn, over a lifetime, to carry a lot of *no* in your body. As your body influences your experience, you create a loop that reinforces the negative. In this practice you break into that loop through your body, thereby introducing a positive influence into your actions and experience.

Without moving, notice carefully how your face feels—the little muscles, their tension and tone. Focus on your forehead, the muscles around your eyes and mouth. Now, step by step, soften your face. That means to do what feels like relaxing these muscles and moving your mouth into a natural smile. Relax your tongue and cheeks. If you have a mirror at hand, it is interesting to watch what happens. Relax your hands and fingers, so they have just enough muscle tone to be graceful. Relax every other part of your body that you notice to be tense. And, of great importance, relax your breath: breathe just a bit more deeply than usual, and as you exhale, make a point of relaxing fully, letting all tension flow out with the breath. Now, whether you are sitting, standing, or lying down, feel your body as poised, balanced, at ease, and positive.

This practice lodges loving deep in your body, so you are loving through and through, rather than just on the surface. Musicians, typists, artists, and others who do precise handwork are often astonished at how much negativity they carry in their hands and body as they approach their main vehicle of expression. Practice this whenever you remember to—when you think about or approach an unloved activity or person, and when you visualize or do any loved activity.

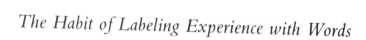

The Habit of Labeling Experience with Words

He who knows does not speak; he who speaks does not know.

LAO TZU

What signifies knowing the names if you know not the Natures of things?

BENJAMIN FRANKLIN

Language, one of the most useful inventions of humanity, takes its toll on loving through the habit of labeling experiences with words. To find a word for something, you do not stand in awe before it, but you compare its features with those of previous experiences whose features have been given names in your language. Your language limits the patterns you can experience to those labeled by its set of words. People long ago identified and labeled all the patterns that a human might experience in your culture. When you arrived, all you had to do to interpret life was learn the patterns and the words that stood for them. In this way, you learned how to be human.

When you label a pattern, you appear to understand it; it

is simply another object with that pattern. A little girl is playing near her father over at the duck pond. She picks up a bright yellow flower and holds it up where the sun turns it into a tiny version of itself. She stands there lost in wonder at the color, the design, the texture, the smell. Then, wanting to *know* what is before her, she runs over and says, "What's this, Daddy?" "That? Why, that's just a dandelion." With a faint little "Oh," she tosses it away, throws into the dirt the little blazing sun, the caressing soft petals, the joyous outpouring of an abundant earth. She knows what it is now—just a dandelion.

You have experienced occasions when your internal labeling was turned off. Perhaps your survival was at stake and the voice did not have time to warm up, or an event was novel or especially moving. You may crave these times and plan recreation and vacation trips to try to create more, not realizing that you can cause them at any time by learning to stop the labeling.

Labeling chops experience up into bits, separates one thing from another, and separates you from the whole. Defining words means drawing boundaries. Labeling puts everything into one pile or another. Once you put an experience in a pile, it becomes like everything else in that pile. Two events have to differ enough to receive different labels in order for you to experience them as different. There are no gradations, no subtleness, nothing new, and nothing wonderful. You sweep the experience into the center of the pile it lies nearest to, so it will be like everything else labeled with that word. It's hard to give a heartfelt yes to one more grassy lawn. But if you can get past the label, you might kneel in awe beside a single blade of grass.

You do not notice what you don't have a word for. For example, you can see more than just people's faces because you have words like *cheek* and *chin*. All too often what has meaning are the categories, the words, the concepts, that reflect people's agreement. Yet words are not the reality; this yellow flower before you now is reality.

Practice 41

CONTRAST EXPERIENCES WITH AND WITHOUT LABELS

A label is a device for classifying experiences, for putting things in pigeon holes. But in the real world pigeon holes do not exist— even the pigeons spend most of their time flying around.

LAURA HUXLEY

Where can I find a man who has forgotten words so I can have a word with him?

CHUANG TZU

Many people actually experience very little, living instead in a haze of mental chatter that distracts them from whatever is at hand. This is an extension of Practice 20, "Attend Without Interpretation." You contrast elements of experiences both with and without the words that label them. Over time, this will enable you to use words only when you choose them for thinking, communication, and deepening experience.

Choose an activity that you particularly enjoy, such as eating an ice cream cone. Take a few minutes and use words to describe that experience. Next, with your eyes closed, imagine eating a whole cone, your favorite flavor. What was that like? Next, actually eat one with no words or memories mixed in. Live in the immediate experience, using all your senses, from the moment you first hold it in your hand until the last taste has faded and you are left with a cool glow from tongue to stomach.

Do some of the perception practices of Chapter 4 while steadfastly refusing to label anything you experience with a word. Listen to the chirping without saying "cricket." Attend to the sky without saying "cloud." Notice how easy or hard it is to do this. Do you crave a label for each new experience? Can you hear the music on the radio without labeling the song, the instruments, the orchestra, the composer? Can you listen to it to enjoy it, or must you fit it into a pigeonhole? Does some word finally jump out and grab the experience? "Yes, that's what it is, a Bach concerto!" Once you have labeled it, how does that affect what you hear?

The Habit of Desiring

> *It is not customary to love what one has.*
> ANATOLE FRANCE

> *The secret waits for the insight of eyes unclouded by longing.*
> LAO TZU

When you desire, you imagine pleasant events into the future and project a powerful yes of hope and anticipation toward them. Because what you want is something you do not have, you can envision it as sweeter than what you do have. The wonderful experience of the unattained awaits a future in which you finally grasp the object of your romanticized love. However, you are surely familiar with attaining at last some powerful desire, only to find the experience far less positive than your fantasies.

Desire is not love. With desire you look right through what is to be loved now. Living in desire, rather than in love, is a way to put loving off into the future, and thus to say no to loving now. The habit keeps you from having to face the obvious fact that all the loving you will ever experience you must experience in some moment of now.

Yet it is a powerful experience to be infatuated with a beloved who is present only in fantasies! Indeed, there have been periods in history, represented by the King Arthur legends, when people restricted love to mean only the desire and not the realization of that desire. They dared not realize their love because they were sure it would destroy their passion—the strong, compelling emotions they considered more important.

When you do achieve a desire, the challenge changes from attaining it to appreciating it. That is a different challenge, one you may not be used to meeting. So you are likely to be disappointed and conclude that you desired the wrong object, that it is time to desire something else. Or you may grow cynical and conclude that satisfaction is impossible and disappointment inevitable.

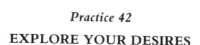

Practice 42

EXPLORE YOUR DESIRES

Listen to desire as you listen to the wind among the trees.

J. KRISHNAMURTI

The mind sees a magnificent pie in the sky; it dwells on it; it wants it; it yearns single-mindedly; the cry for more is endless.

SAI BABA

List in your journal the objects or events that you remember wanting intensely in your life. For each item, recall how you felt as the time for attaining it drew near and finally arrived, or as you realized you would never attain it. For those items you attained, what was the payoff? How deeply could you appreciate or delight in the item you wanted so much? What skills of loving did you display when you turned your desire into joy? What skills of loving did you lack when you failed to turn your desire into the joy you expected?

List the major desires that you have now—not just items that you think it would be nice to have, but items for which your wishes are so strong that they pull you away from the moment and into the future. In each case, are you willing to do what you can to attain the item, trust the future either to give it to you or not, and spend your time appreciating what you have in your life now rather than living in the future?

Practice 43

CELEBRATE SOMETHING NOW

Who is rich? He who rejoices in his portion.

TALMUD

Torah is given to man so he may celebrate life and everything that makes life a source of celebration.

REBBE AVRAHIM KALISKER

In order to experience satisfaction, stop wanting and attend to what you have right now. Celebration is a heartwarming experience that breaks the habit of wanting, because you have to be in the presence of that which you celebrate. Even if you are celebrating a past event, you have to re-create it in your mind in order to celebrate it. Whenever you find yourself lost in fantasies of how great life would be if only some condition were different or you had something that you want, it is time for a celebration!

Determine that you are going to celebrate something—right now, today, or, at the very least, this week. Ask yourself, "What is in my life to celebrate?" Stay with the question until you have an answer. If you cannot think of an answer, you are looking for something too sensational. Make a list of your blessings and celebrate one of them. If you cannot think of any, make a list of things you would miss if they were taken away, and celebrate one of them.

How will you celebrate? With other people? To whom will you communicate your celebration? You can invite people to a celebration event without even knowing yet what you are going to celebrate. The atmosphere of celebration is contagious, and people are happy to join in creating one if for no other reason than that the sun is shining or it is raining, whichever you prefer.

Desires, like preferences, are not *bad*; they motivate your choices and commitments. In order to engage fully and enthusiastically in life, put some passion into your desires. But balance caring deeply about the fruit to come with delighting in the flower before you now. There are always flowers before you, regardless of circumstances. The fruit may never come, and you can still love deeply.

You might refuse to put passion into a desire because you fear you will not get it and do not want the pain of disappointment. But disappointment is only as negative as you make it. Attaining one desire makes it easy to conclude that you *should* attain another. When you know that you will fill your life with love even without the current desire, the possibility of disappointment will not seem so awful.

Weak wanting can lead to an ambiguous life, a flat, boring existence in which nothing seems to make any difference. To accomplish useful service and give passion and guidance to your life, throw yourself into some of your desires. Yet to avoid the trap of desires, carry them lightly, without dramatizing how wonderful life will be if you achieve them or how terrible it will be if you do not.

Practice 44

SLOW DOWN AND GO DEEPLY INTO A SINGLE EXPERIENCE

As it is, we are merely bolting our lives—gulping down undigested experiences as fast as we can stuff them in—because awareness of our own existence is so superficial and so narrow that nothing seems to us more boring than simple being.

ALAN WATTS

When you want what you get, you've always got what you want, because you've always got what you get.

MOUNTAIN VIEW ZEN CENTER

Notice occasions when you typically run from one desired object or activity to another, one stimulus to the next, bolting them down. Ask yourself what you are really wanting that you are not getting by flitting from desire to desire. A visit to the zoo might be an example, as you hurry from one cage to the next, trying not to miss anything. The next time, stop running and pay attention to only one object or activity. Watch the ring-tailed cats for the next two hours. How much can you learn about them? How much can you empathize with them, delight in them, feel at one with them, be amused by them?

Ask yourself whether your own achievements are examples of hurrying from one desire to the next. As soon as you reach some desired goal, do you take it for granted and never stop to acknowledge yourself and appreciate what you have done, but immediately rush on to achieve the next item on your list of desires? Is the result a greed for accomplishments and a lack of satisfaction and delight in living? If so, again go deeply into an individual accomplishment, attend to the nuances of what you have done or are doing, appreciate it, celebrate it.

The Demand for Ownership

Whoever forces it spoils it. Whoever grasps it loses it.

LAO TZU

In our acquisitive society people equate love with ownership. To own something means that for a time it is in your presence and society lets you make decisions regarding it. Societies set up rules of ownership in order to keep people from quarreling over who can do what.

But deep inside you know you do not own anything. You may be the steward of many things, a caretaker for a while, but at any moment what you love could be pulled away from you. You cannot be secure in owning or clinging to what you love. Indeed, clutching the beloved expresses and increases your fear of losing it. Security comes not from hanging on to love objects, but from being able to turn whatever comes your way into one.

Practice 45

WHAT DO YOU REALLY OWN?

The situation of the soul in contemplation is something like the situation of Adam and Eve in paradise. Everything is yours, but on one infinitely important condition: that it is all given. There is nothing that you can claim, nothing that you can demand, nothing that you can take. And as soon as you try to take something as if it were your own—you lose your Eden.

THOMAS MERTON

In this practice you explore the notion of ownership, inquiring into what you tell yourself you own and what that ownership means. It will help you avoid clutching or grasping for love objects and lead to greater appreciation, respect, and awe for the many that are already present in your life.

Make a list of classes of objects that you own. What does that ownership mean? That is, what is present in a relationship that leads you to say you own something? For each item, ask if you are free to do whatever you choose with the object. Ask if it will remain in your possession forever. Ask if you have any obligation toward it in order to justify your ownership.

Notice for each item how easily it could be pulled away from you. Clothes? They wear out, tear, and get lost or stained. Your faculties? Suppose you had a stroke. A tree in your yard? It could die of drought or disease. Children? They grow up. A spouse? You could be divorced or widowed.

Since you cannot truly *own* a loved one, how does the concept of ownership serve your loving purpose? How might you better view your relationships with the items on your list?

O my God, how does it happen in this poor old world that Thou art so great and yet nobody finds Thee, that Thou callest so loudly and nobody hears Thee, that Thou art so near and nobody feels Thee, that Thou givest Thyself to everybody and nobody knows Thy name? Men flee from Thee and say they cannot find Thee; they turn their backs and say they cannot see Thee; they stop their ears and say they cannot hear Thee.

HANS DENK

7 ❧ LOVING OUTLOOKS ON LIFE

Be content with what you have; rejoice in the way things are. When you realize there is nothing lacking, the whole world belongs to you.

LAO TZU

Love bears all things, believes all things . . . endures all things. Love never ends.

ST. PAUL

*I*t is not so hard to respond to life with love when the circumstances are to your liking. But, no matter how hard you work to control those circumstances, they will not always be to your liking. Indeed, sometimes you will dislike them intensely. It is easy to nod your head to these statements of Lao tzu and St. Paul, but not so easy to figure out how to "bear all things, believe all things, endure all things."

Fortunately for us, through the centuries, people have tried a lot of methods of doing just that. Certain approaches to life that work well in diverse cultures have been discovered and rediscovered through many millennia. Living from one of these vantage points is really refining a mindfulness practice similar to that of Practice 27, in which you predetermine a loving position from which you experience the events around you. From this position, you are able to keep from being distracted by the inevitable events that you do not like, and to give a deeper *yes* to all events.

Watch Life as a River

> *Be in the world but not of the world.*
> JESUS

> *The dogs bark; the caravan passes.*
> ARABIC SAYING

The physical world consists of matter and the forms imposed on that matter. Over time, the forms come, change, and go. Your body, your friends and loved ones, locations, jobs, abilities, and opportunities—all come, change, and go. If you see these comings, changings, and goings as threats to your security, you will respond with fear. If you see them as moments of mystery being unveiled before your eyes, you will respond with love: "What is this? Oh, yes." "And now what is this? Ah, yes."

Practice 46

CULTIVATE THE ROLE OF OBSERVER

The yogi then looked on, mentally unperturbed, at the interminable flow of thoughts as though he were tranquillity, resting on the shore of a river watching the water flow past.

PADMA–KARPO

This is the practice of seeing life as a river, bearing now this twig, now this rose blossom, now this gum wrapper, now this child, always flowing before you. First spend some time sitting on the bank of a real stream or river and meditate on it. Watch it to see what is there simply as a moment of mystery being revealed to you, and to know the river as a metaphor for life. If there is no stream or river nearby, attend to the flight of birds through the trees, watch the river of cars drive by your house, listen to the flow of music, or to the playful cries of kids in the park.

Extend this outlook to all of life. This practice in

observation differs from the appreciation exercise, Practice 30, since its purpose is to observe rather than appreciate what the river of life brings. If you sometimes add the element of appreciation to the practice, remember you are committed to appreciating it *all*— the gum wrapper as much as the rose blossom. If you find you are not ready to do that yet, then just watch it all float by, with no judgments, no evaluations, no labeling. Just sit by the stream of life and see what it offers. What mystery is being unveiled at this moment? This moment—now.

❦ ─────────────────────────────── ❦

Speak a Loving Internal Voice

All that we are is the result of what we thought.

BUDDHA

The world is such-and-such or so-and-so only because we tell ourselves that that is the way it is.

DON JUAN (CARLOS CASTANEDA)

If you are like most people, much of the time you are hypnotized by your internal voices. Sometimes they pronounce a crisis—"How awful! This is terrible!" Sometimes they pronounce that someone, perhaps you, is inadequate, wrong, or no good. Notice how compelling those voices are, bestowing truth, exaggerating the importance of success and failure, and telling you what you must do. Listen to them prattle away, one after another, like the sound of a river rolling through your mind, some saying one thing and some another.

Just because a voice speaks in your mind does not make it true. Even if your experience confirms it, that does not mean you would have the same experience if you took the voice less seriously. Language does more than just describe, even when it is most descriptive. Language always *evokes*.

If you have acted in plays, you know how easily your lines evoke your experience. So use words deliberately to evoke love. Declare your relationship, your love, even when the circumstances do not put you in a loving mood.

Practice 47

REPEAT A LOVING MANTRA

And if you desire to have this intent (to reach God) summarized in one word, take but a little word of one syllable. And such a word is LOVE—*and fasten this word to your heart so it may never go away no matter what befalls you. And if any thought presses on you to ask what you would have, answer with just this one word.*

THE CLOUD OF UNKNOWING

When you say something like ("I love you") with your whole being, not just with your mouth or your intellect, it can transform the world. A statement that has such power of transformation is called a mantra.

THICH NHAT HANH

I come into the living room to play the piano before dinner and notice Elizabeth asleep on the sofa. I pick up a version of the Brahms lullaby that I especially like. As I sit down at the keyboard I say to myself, "I love you, Elizabeth," putting as much feeling into the words as I can. As I raise my hands to the keys I repeat silently, "I love you, Elizabeth." As I start to play, I begin a process that spirals between caressing her with my hands at the keyboard and the sound of the music and my internal voice. Into each—hands, sound, and voice—I pour as much tenderness and care as I can, and each evokes more tenderness and care in the others. Though she never wakes up during the entire piece, now that I have loved Elizabeth that deeply, my life and my relationship with her are changed forever.

In this practice, you go beyond witnessing your internal voices and deliberately pick one to speak, over and over, to further you along your loving path. You choose a word or expression that reminds you of your path, and you repeat it as a mantra silently to yourself as you go about your daily life. This interrupts the usual train of voices, changes your rhythms, and holds you to your purpose. You tend to be what you fill your mind with.

Be creative and try different mantras under the different circumstances of your life. You may or may not want to refer to a higher power like God; you may or may not want to use archaic language. Here are some examples of mantras that have been effective for many people.

I love you.	Here is the thing that God has willed for me.
I love this.	This is my path—this!
I am at peace.	This is what I was meant for.
God, I thank thee!	I choose love here, I choose love.
I am here to love.	Yes!
So be it.	Amen.
Rejoice!	How beautiful!

If, for example, you use "I love you" as a mantra, think it over and over as powerfully and as meaningfully as you can. Use it when you approach a romantic partner or the students in your class or your colleagues or customers at work, when you pet your cat or feed your fish, when you are keeping a bedside vigil for someone who is sick, when you listen to a bird or feel the warmth of the sun, when you see your reflection in the mirror or remember your grandmother or the boyfriend you had when you were thirteen, or when you are talking to your daughter on the phone. Say it to the person you see in your rearview mirror driving the car behind you when you are stopped at a stoplight.

As another example, say "God, I thank thee!" even before you know what you have to be thankful for. As a declaration it forces you to look around to see what you might experience in a thankful way. It frees you from taking everything for granted, from acknowledging only the most unusual blessings.

Play Life as a Game

Work consists of whatever a body is obliged to do. Play consists of whatever a body is not obliged to do.

MARK TWAIN

Angels can fly because they take themselves lightly.

G. K. CHESTERTON

Work is activity directed toward some end or goal, and we think of its value or meaning as lying in reaching that end. A game may also take the form of getting from where you are to a goal. But you *play* a game, which means the goal is not the real purpose. Play is now-oriented, toward the joy or love of the moment. A game becomes work when you play it only for winning. Life, viewed as a whole, must be a game, since the end of life is death and you will die without taking away any of the points or goals.

Do not confuse the score of a game as measured by making goals with its real purpose. You can win money, fame, spouse, children and thus reach your goals. But when you set out on a path of loving, you determine to play for joy, for love, not just to work for money or fame.

When you play a game, even if you do not like the rules, you have agreed to them, so you do not fight them. The rules are, of course, arbitrary, existing only by agreement among those playing. Choosing to play life as a loving game, you choose whatever events come up as part of that game, even if you do not like some of them.

Practice 48

CULTIVATE THE ROLE OF PLAYER

The Fifth (and only) Rule: You have taken yourself too seriously.
                                                    ARTHUR BLOCH

This practice is to live life consciously as a game, using your own sense of what that means to guide you in responding to circumstances. You dance down the street for no reason other than that you said you would and you are alive on a beautiful planet full of wonderful creatures. You hold the crises of your life in the same way you would hold setbacks or losses in any other game.

Playing life as a game does not mean trivializing life. There is nothing trivial about the game of your life— it affects the circumstances in which everyone lives. To love a game, you must play it hard, with your whole heart—yet when you lose, you shrug and go back to play the next day.

Can you live totally engaged in what you are doing, without clinging to the outcome, the score? Can you experience life as both serious and absurd at the same time? Can you be in pain at one level, and at another level be happy because you are playing a wonderful game?

You win the game of life if you play the whole way with caring and enthusiasm. Your goals are just the excuse to play. The plays and players that pop up in the game are the raw material for your loving. Respect your fellow players. Even though they drop a few balls, they, like you, are in the big league.

View Life as a Drama

All the world's a stage, and all the men and women merely players.
WILLIAM SHAKESPEARE

When you are acting in or watching a play, you know that the whole show is happening so that you and the rest of the people can love it. When you are onstage, you pour yourself into your roles, using them as vehicles for putting loving energy and care into the world. When you take your seat in the audience, you can witness the play in safety, loving every gesture and learning from every moment.

Practice 49

BE BOTH ROLE-PLAYER AND SPECTATOR

Any role becomes a trap if you take it seriously.
RAM DASS

This practice is to live life consciously as a theatrical drama. Cultivate a vantage point inside yourself where you are a spectator who can witness whatever is going on, even in difficult times. Since you are safe sitting in that seat in the audience, you are free when you want to get up on stage and throw yourself into your roles wholeheartedly. Choose your roles with care as ways to express your aliveness. Though you play them with your whole heart, never identify your *self* with what happens to the roles you play.

It is easy to get so caught up in the drama that you think *you* are one of your roles. You are not—you are the one who plays the roles, and also the one who watches the whole drama. You may *choose to step* into a play in which to act, you can intend to marry the hero and live happily ever after. But you do not *have* to in order to live happily, because it is still a wonderful play and your part is so exciting.

Trust Life and the World

> *Love is letting go of fear.*
> GERALD JAMPOLSKY

> *Fear tells you, "I want to make you safe." Love says, "You* are *safe."*
> EMMANUEL (PAT RODEGAST)

It is not easy to be a human. You are born helpless, cared for by inexperienced and fallible people who hold your life in their hands. You are born without an instruction manual, so you are taught the purpose of your life, your limitations, your worth, by these and other fallible people who know precious little about life. Your body is most likely of only average attractiveness and capabilities, and it disconcerts you by its illnesses, injuries, cravings, aging, and inevitable movement toward death. You and everyone else continually disappoint each other, you make mistakes. You live as one of many in an overcrowded world that gives lots of criticism and little acknowledgment, so it is hard to feel that you make a positive difference to others.

Given all this, it is understandable if you have learned to focus on the negative events in your life in an effort to avoid them and thereby formed the habit of fearing. When you fear, you project unpleasant events into an uncertain future and direct a powerful *no* toward them. You are so concerned over possible trouble in the future that you overlook whatever is lovable in your life now.

Fear comes when you refuse to trust. You do not have to trust only in reaction to circumstances that seem trustworthy. Your future may not seem worthy of being trusted. It may seem fraught with danger, but you can trust it intentionally anyway. There is something both wonderful and poignant about deliberately trusting that the universe knows what it is doing in creating you and your fellow beings, even though your plight includes inevitable aging, loss, and death. Trust is a stance you take toward life and the world, one in which you know the truth about what the future could contain, but a stance that says you will cope with painful events when they occur and in the meantime will love as deeply as you can.

Practice 50

EXPLORE YOUR FEARS

Human life is a schoolroom. Take the curriculum.

EMMANUEL (PAT RODEGAST)

> *You are a child of the universe,*
> *No less than the trees and the stars;*
> *You have a right to be here.*
> *And whether or not it is clear to you,*
> *No doubt the universe*
> *Is unfolding as it should.*

DESIDERATA (MAX EHRMANN)

Think through your life and list the events or conditions that you actually experience fear about. List only items that you actively fear, not ones that you know intellectually might prove negative. For each of these events or conditions, write out what it is you distrust about yourself or the world that leads to this fear. It may be that you do not trust your strength to bear pain, or society's willingness to care for you in time of need, or the wisdom of a world that made you and your fellow creatures mortal.

If you hold human life to be a schoolroom, then a major part of the curriculum is whatever set of difficulties your circumstances present. What would it take for you to trust what you do not trust now? What actions could you take that would make it easier to trust? Take those actions. For example, develop a support network of friends and relatives, or draw up a living will if that would make you feel you could approach old age with more trust.

Regardless of whether you are willing to trust the world at this time, turn your attention to something other than your fears. The world has countless places you can put your energy, countless objects you can love. Get your attention off of yourself and onto something outside you. You need not live in fear.

 ——————————————————————————

If by patience, if by watching, . . . the world which was dead prose to me become living and divine, shall I not watch ever? Shall I not be a watchman henceforth?

HENRY DAVID THOREAU

8 ❦ LOVING OTHER PEOPLE

Thou shalt love thy neighbor as thyself.
JESUS

I never met a man I didn't like.
WILL ROGERS

People constantly challenge your ability to love. Sometimes they make it easy for you, but often what they do seems to get in the way of love. In this chapter you prepare for and practice loving encounters with other people, be they the most intimate members of your family or someone you only glimpse at a distance. You will learn to use your relationships with people as bountiful sources of loving experiences instead of as sources of frustrations. Increasingly, you will bring satisfaction to your relationships, rather than try to get it from them.

The Purpose of Relationships

We have only ourselves and one another.
That may not be much, but that's all there is.
SHELLY KOPP

You are free at any moment to choose the purpose of your relationship with another person. Of course, the practical goals of child bearing and raising, wage-earning, and life support that you associate with family, friends, co-workers, and the many people you interact with as you conduct your daily business, will be staring you in the face.

You can let the fulfillment of those practical goals be the purpose of your relationships: You and your daughter can cook supper so you can eat in time to get the dishes done before it is too late to do the ironing before you have to go to bed. . . .

It is easy to let the practical needs dictate the relationship's purpose and live your whole life just getting things done. Soon your daughter grows up and leaves home and you realize that in all the hassle you forgot to love living with her.

While your goal may be doing something as practical as getting supper on the table, you may hold different purposes for the relationship: as an invitation to *love the other*, as a challenge to *love your own life*, as an arena for *learning to love*, as an opportunity to *learn about another* person, as an opportunity to *learn about yourself.* In order to cultivate the art and practice of loving, you can make each of your relationships a mindfulness exercise of holding to these purposes, shifting among them from time to time as circumstances warrant.

Practice 51

MAKE LOVING THE PURPOSE OF YOUR RELATIONSHIPS

Who is wise? He who learns from all men.
TALMUD

I believe in person to person; every person is Christ for me, and since there is only one Jesus, that person is the one person in the world at that moment.
MOTHER TERESA

Pick one of the important people in your life and assert that the primary purpose of your relationship is to love that person. Of course, you will work at practical goals together, depending on the nature of your relationship. But whenever you are with or thinking about the person, your priority is to have the heart-warming experiences of loving. (Specific techniques are presented later in this chapter.)

This practice keeps your priorities clear. Over time, you will improve your skills at loving, love your own life more, and learn more about that person and about yourself. Whenever you find yourself off purpose and you cannot resume a loving stance, use that as a signal to learn: "What can I learn about this person and about me from this incident?" Avoid blaming either of you or labeling anyone right or wrong. You are committed to two primary purposes—loving and learning.

Broaden this practice to the other people in your life, ranging from parents, spouse, and children, to the person behind the checkout counter at the grocery store. In this way, you can gain skill at this mindfulness exercise throughout your life as you practice it. There is no limit to how powerfuly you can learn to love the people with whom you live.

 ————————————————————————

Love for Love's Sake

You're not "in love with her," but "in love with life by way of her."

STEWART EMERY

You can love only humans, not humanity. To love at all, you must love a specific person or event. You may be romantically attracted to countless people, but at any moment you do your romantic loving with one unique person. Without this one, you could not express romantic love. The specific person, the specific sunset, the specific job, the specific flower, the specific idea—these are the samples the universe offers you. You get to love these samples, and only through them do you get to love at all.

An ancient image is that you are a musician and love is the song you are put here to play. As a flute player, you can mistakenly attribute your music to your particular flute, becoming overly attached to it or blaming it for times when the music is disappointing. Your flute is not your song of love; it is the vehicle through which you play that song.

When you love an individual, you respond to his jet-black hair and the way he tosses his head. But if you make that hair or toss of the head the *reason* for your love, you confuse the flute with the song. Love his hair, yet love him for the sake of love, not for the sake of his hair. It will soon turn gray. The reason you love is that you are determined to play this song of love and you have chosen him, at this moment, to be your flute.

Practice 52

LOVE LIFE THROUGH THIS INDIVIDUAL

God is not love. God is not loving.
God is someone loving something, or something loving
  someone.

R. H. BLYTH

In this practice when you interact with a person, you consciously pour your love, your care, your awe for all of life and the world into this single action with this single person. This will enhance the meaning of each word, each touch, from a gesture to a caress of the universe.

Practice this further in activities that do not involve people. Mow the lawn as a loving touch to groom the earth, which has supported life for over four billion years, has sustained your ancestors, and now nourishes you. Pet your cat as a way of expressing love to all animals, and indeed to all of life. Let her warm, purring softness stand for all the nurturing mammals of millions of years that prepared earth for your life, and be grateful that you have this affectionate vehicle through which to express your care and thanks. When you next cook a meal, engage in a uniquely human action of love and service whereby you transform an assortment of unlikely products into nourishment for yourself and those you love. Brush your teeth as a way of caring for your body and thereby caring for all living bodies.

The Art and Practice of Intimacy

Love turns upon a commitment to a certain kind of seeing, a certain kind of sharing.

ROBERT C. SOLOMON

Some aspects of loving we call *intimacy*—being connected, mutually at one, sharing an attention, interest, and enthusiasm for each other that goes deeper than the surface. Intimacy is an *approach* you take to another—that of attention and openness. Of course, you can wait until the circumstances are so powerful, as in sexual activity, that you have no choice but to react with attention and openness. Such waiting will mean that you rarely experience intimacy. However, you can use attention and openness as a mindfulness practice and achieve intimacy with anyone you wish.

Some people may not want intimacy, confusing it with sexual activity because they have experienced so little intimacy in nonsexual settings. Some people may not want intimacy because they fear that the other person will find them wanting. Be sensitive to those concerns, but do not let them stop you. Just practice intimacy in ways and with people where it is appropriate.

Practice 53

THIRTEEN TECHNIQUES FOR PRACTICING INTIMACY

To love somebody is not just a strong feeling—it is a decision, it is a judgment, it is a promise.

ERICH FROMM

The first duty of love is to listen.
PAUL TILLICH

This is the practice of intimacy in all relationships where intimacy is appropriate. That means relationships with close friends, siblings, parents, children, grandchildren, and in both the nonsexual and sexual aspects of romantic relationships.

Notice how the very name of this practice suggests sexual activity because few people experience intimacy without the powerful motivation of sex. Work to separate intimacy from sex in your mind, so that you will be able to make not only your sexual activities more intimate, but your nonsexual activities as well.

The individual steps of this practice are in themselves powerful practices for deepening any love—during a committee meeting, a telephone call, writing a letter, or attending to your pet hamster.

The practice of intimacy is a mindfulness exercise in which your purpose is to be open and honest with your partner and to pay scrupulous attention to him or her. With practice you will find your own ways to increase intimacy with different people, but here are some universal techniques. You can practice these skills singly or any number of them together.

1. Willfully appreciate this person, whether you are together or not. Appreciation is a doorway into the heart.

2. Commit the time you are together to attending to this person, and forget the other things you could be doing. After all, *this* is the person you are with right now. So make him or her the right one. *This is it!* This one. Now. Don't look over your shoulder to see who else is around, don't miss feeling your partner's presence now while you are together.

3. Silently send love to your partner. Say inside your head, "I love you," while you look at him or her and really mean what you say. You can learn to say "I love you" quietly in

your head with so much feeling that you *evoke* the experience of love.

4. Look into your partner's eyes, especially when you speak. Looking into someone's eyes, the "windows of the soul," can distract you from your thoughts if you have not practiced doing it. You or your partner may experience discomfort at the increased intimacy. Remember your purpose. These are techniques of love, not of manipulation or assertiveness.

5. Look intently at your partner—when he or she speaks or even in silence. Looking lowers barriers. There is no negative connotation to not looking, but by not looking you miss a major way of connecting with each other.

6. Give subtle positive feedback (nod, smile, agree) whenever your partner evaluates himself or herself positively.

7. Speak what is on your mind, in particular your feelings. Some people rarely talk about their feelings and may not even be aware of them. Others talk so easily about how they feel that their friends wish they would change the subject. Work toward a happy medium in your own relationships.

8. Share a triumph. A triumph is any event you are willing to interpret as a triumph and describe from that interpretation. Triumph sharing breaks the pattern of complaining that makes up so much conversation. If you schedule time for mutual triumph sharing, you will regularly scan your experience for the positive. Families can regularly start dinner by having everyone share a triumph of the day.

9. Ask for what you want, in particular for loving or caring actions. Do not empower the voice that says that you can delight in behavior only when it is spontaneous and unrequested. This practice is deepened if at the

moment you make your request, you picture in your mind a time when you gave to someone else what you are asking for. Since you cannot control what your partner does, he or she may not give you what you want. In that case, stay with what you can control, namely holding to your purpose, which is to practice intimacy.

10. Sense, ask, or listen attentively for what is wanted from you, and give it, so long as it is in keeping with your values and with practicing intimacy.

11. No matter how familiar you may be, put what you know about this person out of your mind and confront him or her afresh. Your images of other people provide you certainty and security, but at the cost of living in the fixed world of your own pictures. Foster a sense of awe for this person—this marvelous form, so fragile and mortal, and yet so tough —through which the energy of the cosmos pours out into your life as you in turn pour such energy into his or her life.

12. From time to time, you will notice your thoughts placing conditions on when you will love. "I could love her (more) if only she . . . ." Just notice those conditions and let them go, turn your attention to something else. Your purpose is *unconditional loving.*

13. Wherever you are, whatever you are doing, reach out for a moment in your awareness and include your partner with you. Form a unit in your mind of the two of you as one. When you are together, silently say, "You are with me," "You are like me," or "You are me." This will help you to experience the couple or the group, rather than the individual. You will see your similarities, rather than stay in the habit of emphasizing your differences.

These practices will show how strong your barriers are to intimacy. You will see how much you protect yourself from others and they from you. You may sense how deeply you fear being caught without this protection. You may even learn what it is you fear, and find that it is not as bad as you thought to have someone experience you as a human being—fallible and scared and wanting to love.

Practice 54

BE WITH SOMEONE

Have you ever really looked anybody in the face?

J. KRISHNAMURTI

This practice in intimacy is simply looking someone in the face while that person looks back at you. The practice overcomes barriers to intimacy, not just with this person, but with anyone. Furthermore, it frees you to be more self-confident and assertive in all your dealings.

Agree with someone to practice being with him for a certain period of time. Set a timer if you have one. While even a moment is valuable, start with ten minutes and increase the duration as you gain experience. Sit a couple of feet opposite your partner. Then simply be with him. Look him in the face while he looks in your face. You are not staring at each other, you are simply being with each other. Don't send him love or worry about what he is feeling or thinking. Don't judge him, just see him, feel his presence. If you find yourself escaping into thoughts or judgments, notice what you are doing and come back to being with him. When the time is up, give your partner a hug.

The first few times you do this practice, you may be surprised by the emotions that come up. You or your partner may feel discomfort, sadness, hilarity, ecstasy, or anguish. You may have an overwhelming desire to break off the practice by speaking, turning away, crying, or laughing. Don't. Just observe what happens and keep up the practice. If you cannot, ask another friend to sit by you, touch you, or put an arm around you, to support you in having the confidence to do the practice. Ask yourself what you can learn from the discomfort you and your partner had in doing this practice. Can you use this practice to offer people more compassion and wisdom?

Practice 55

TOUCH ANOTHER THROUGH YOUR HAND

Remember that the Holy Spirit interprets the body only as a means of communication (of love).

A COURSE IN MIRACLES

Attention is the food of love. To foster loving (positive) experience, develop positive attention. When you shake hands or hold hands with someone, what do you feel? A hand? No, you feel a pattern of warmth and pressure that you *infer* to be skin, to be a hand. What you infer from such a pattern of warmth and pressure is up to you. You can shake hands with someone, hug, even have sex, and yet not *touch* him or her, the person inside that body, the soul. To touch, you have to create that meaning. *You* have to come into your hand and reach through to *them*. This practice in placing your attention will give you the ability to caress the world by touching it, and to be caressed by it in return.

Take someone's hand and feel simply the pattern of warmth and pressure that it creates. Now be aware of her skin touching yours to make that pattern. Next, feel through your hand the life/energy/love in the person you are touching. Let that life/energy/love move into you, and let your own move into her. Now, without changing your grip, feel your hand on hers as a loving caress of her. As you caress her through your hand, be caressed by her through it in return. With your hands in each other's, touch more than just hands—touch each other. *You* touch *her* through your hand. Practice moving your attention from the usual, safe, just-shaking-hands grip to an intimate caress, without moving your fingers in the least.

Put your heart in your hand and stretch it out to touch the world. Touch anything and communicate from your heart to it. Pet your dog or cat, sending your love to it, and through it to the universe whose energy it represents. Caress with your touch your musical instrument, sports equipment, or the tools of your profession or trade. If you kiss someone, kiss *that person* through your lips. If you have sex with someone, love *that person* through your body. This is why people have bodies—to touch the world with love.

Practice 56

PAINT ANOTHER WITH LOVE

Do you want to know what's in my heart?
From the beginning of time: just this! just this!
RYŌKAN

The act of caressing does not require that you touch someone physically. There are countless ways, such as through your eyes or your voice. An action becomes a caress through the spirit you bring to it—through your making it a touch of love. In painting another with love you forgo physical touch in order to practice the inner work of creating the loving spirit. What you learn thereby you can apply to any caress you choose to make.

The person you will paint needs only to stand (or sit or lie) quietly for perhaps ten or fifteen minutes. Your paintbrush will be one or both of your hands, which you will keep at least a half-inch, perhaps as much as six inches, from the person's body. The physical act of painting, which is so like a caress, will feed back in to you to evoke a deeper experience of love. Your challenge is to see how much awe, wonder, appreciation, and tenderness you can experience and paint onto your partner using your hands as paintbrushes. Experience for yourself how wonderful this creature truly is, and paint that love onto your partner through a couple inches of air.

You may feel silly at first, and your efforts may seem stiff and without feeling. Don't worry. Expert performers on any instrument start as awkward beginners. Unless you and your partner plan to use the practice as part of sexual activity, determine to yourself in advance that you are not here for sexual purposes, that you will keep your hands away from sexual areas of the body, and that if sexual feeling arises in you, you will move your attention away from it.

Painting someone with love is a creative act on your part, a way of expressing and evoking your deepest feelings toward the universe that has made you. Practice it with anyone with whom you are willing to experience intimacy. Some people find that being painted with love increases their energy or vitality, makes them more positive, relieves pain, or benefits them in other ways.

Of course, you can paint any object with love, from your late husband's picture to your dog or your plants, as long as you can practice caressing it honestly. It is never a question of how objectively loveworthy the object is. Loving is not the assessment of objective worth. It is always a question of how deeply you can evoke a *yes* toward this object.

Express Your Love

> *Spread your thoughts of love beyond limits.*
> **BUDDHA**

When you experience the heartwarmings of love, tell someone about it. Saying it ratifies it for you, keeps you from losing it, warms the lives of those you tell, and makes a world in which love is more valued and supported, and thus more commonly experienced. It takes determination to put messages of love out into a world that is caught up in how bad things are. But you can do it, and over time you are likely to be appreciated for doing it. After all, most people believe in loving; they just want the other fellow to begin first.

Practice 57

WRITE OUT A CARESS

Pick a person who is or has been important in your life and write out the most powerful appreciation of him or her that you can. Identify and describe what you most appreciate about this person, how he or she has affected your life for the better. This is for your journal only; if later you want to show it to the person, that is a separate matter. Your purpose in this practice is to experience the spiraling effect as feeling evokes writing, which evokes deeper feeling . . . all leading to a written record and a powerfully loving experience that adds to your relationship. This is a chance to let go—to be as poetic, as mushy, as emphatic as you can be. Let the pen on the paper, asking for words to write, entice you into searching your experience for creative ways to appreciate the other person.

This practice is valuable, though your subject may have died or left you years ago. It creates new interpretations, new stories, to replace or stand alongside the old. Direct this practice at nonhuman subjects as well, an animal, plant, job, possession, house, town, country, the earth—anything for which you are willing to cultivate the experience of love.

Practice 58

HOW MANY WAYS CAN YOU SAY I LOVE YOU?

How do you say "I love you?" Often, and loud!

LEO BUSCAGLIA

This practice is an experiment in which you see how many ways you can express your love to the people in your life. The practice will increase your repertoire of methods so you will be able to love often, yet appropriately, so that people will accept your message. It also will make you more sensitive to how others express love to you.

In your journal note down when in the past day you have communicated love to others. To whom did you communicate it and how? Communications do not have to be verbal. What about the bathroom mirror you washed, that cat dish you refilled, or the smile you gave the new woman at the office?

Pay attention to others to see how they express love, and learn from them. Some people never learn to say "I love you" directly, so they beat around the bush by asking, "How's your car running these days?" Or, "Are you pregnant yet?" Warm the way you listen to others communicate, to see if they might be expressing love, the strongest expression they are capable of at the moment.

Think over the many people in your life and imagine how you could express to each of them your appreciation, delight, or other aspect of your experience of *yes*. Determine to express that love to them the next time it is appropriate. When you do, note the event in your journal.

If you block yourself and do not say it when the time is ripe, examine the negative thoughts that blocked you. Challenge the truth of those thoughts. Is it really true, for example, that if you expressed ap-

preciation to the custodian for cleaning the floor, he
would think you were crazy? Try it and see.

Practice 59

STAY UP TO DATE IN EXPRESSING APPRECIATION

*To be properly expressed a thing must proceed from within, moved
by its form: it must come, not in from without but out from within.*
MEISTER ECKHART

A lot of people play and have played important roles
in your life. Time is passing, and you will not have
forever to acknowledge them. To express your gratitude for the positive role they have played, to let them
know how they enriched and benefited you, acknowledge them now. Live so that if you were to die at any
moment, you would know that you had communicated your thanks and love to everyone you wanted
to. Keep yourself up to date in expressing appreciation.

Think over your life and recall people who have
meant a lot to you. To whom have you fully expressed
your appreciation? Begin to communicate with them
by phone and mail and in person to let them know.
Rather than buying printed greeting cards for holidays
or anniversaries, write letters saying how much your
relationship with the person means to you.

Remember to express appreciation throughout the
day whenever it seems appropriate. Set a target of so
many people per day that you will compliment.

As a challenging experiment, walk right up to someone and say, "I want to express my appreciation to
you right now . . . " without knowing before you
start what you are going to say.

If you have lost physical contact with someone, or
if someone has died, you can still express appreciation.
Remember them as vividly as you can and think, talk,
or write to them.

When you radiate love, do it not to make anyone

feel better, not so someone will think better of you, not to be a nice person. Do it for the same reason that the sun shines, that the rose blooms, that the mockingbird sings—as an outflowing of the loving energy of the universe.

Practice 60

NURTURE YOUR MAJOR RELATIONSHIPS

Love is what you've been through with somebody.

JAMES THURBER

As you share activities with someone, you build a relationship together, which exists in your memories of the events you have shared. Your choice of shared activities provides the raw material for these memories. Take care, therefore, to nurture your relationships by spending time doing positive things together so that the memories will be easy to appreciate. Avoid laying down negative memories that will get in the way.

This is the practice of sitting down and thinking seriously about each of your major relationships to see how much you are nurturing it. How much time do you spend together—in person, by phone, by mail? What is the quality of attention that you have for each other during that time? What is the balance between pleasant and unpleasant events that you share? How could you assert yourself to make the relationship more positive, more intimate, more mutually nurturing, so that it will live in memories that are easy to love?

Then talk it over with the other person, to work out an agreement to make the relationship more positive, more loving. When you carry through on the agreement, acknowledge yourselves for taking the quality of your relationship into your own hands and nurturing it, rather than just trusting it to luck. Asserting that kind of responsibility pays off in a loving, satisfying life.

Not all your relationships are loving. Indeed, some of them may draw you into such negative memories that you have little time or energy for anything positive. How you can bring peace to those relationships is what we will examine next.

Spread love everywhere you go: first of all in your own home. Give love to your children, to your wife or husband, to a next door neighbor. . . . Let no one ever come to you without leaving better and happier. Be the living expression of God's kindness; kindness in your face, kindness in your eyes, kindness in your smile, kindness in your warm greeting.

MOTHER TERESA

9 ❦ KEEPING YOUR RELATIONSHIPS AT PEACE

To be wronged is nothing unless you continue to remember it.

CONFUCIUS

Love thy neighbor, even when he plays the trombone.

JEWISH SAYING

*W*ar in a relationship means a heartfelt *no*. In a warring relationship, negative memories draw your attention to this person again and again, thus blocking you from loving him and diverting you from loving anyone or anything else.

This chapter contains a series of practices to bring peace to a relationship as soon as you notice the negativity, to end fear, anger, hurt, regret, resentment, blame, shame, and guilt. The benefits—learning the lessons the relationship offers, freeing yourself to move on, and uncovering the love that may be hidden there—are worth the work.

Relationships—Warring and Peaceful

What was is the death of what is. . . . To understand is to live with "what is"; which does not mean to be contented with "what is." On the contrary.

J. KRISHNAMURTI

Many of your relationships are transactions fixed by your roles with people: child, parent, sibling, pupil, teacher, colleague, sex partner, spouse, baseball player, worker, consumer, provider. In each of these relationships there have been many occasions when you and the other party hurt and disappointed each other. Your parents and siblings were only the first to offer you relationships containing pain and disappointment, in which both they and you made mistakes, some costly.

In order to love the people in your life more deeply, you will have to do so in spite of vivid memories of times they have been unlovable. People find many ways to hurt one another. When hurt, you experience the pain, you interpret it, often dramatically, and you remember it. You cling to your memories of what they did to you, of what you did back, and of what it all means. You resent them and blame them—and yourself.

War in a relationship keeps you from living every moment afresh, because remembering or seeing the other person triggers mechanical reactions of denial, anger, blame, depression, guilt, how-could-I, how-could-you, if-only, regret, resentment, righteousness, sadness, shame, powerlessness, and wrongness. Your conflict separates you from the other person, and by getting caught up in being right or wrong you can justify even the most destructive behavior.

It seems impossible to love people who hurt and disappoint us. Yet there are no other kinds of people. Ultimately, people are neither good nor bad—people are human. One of the skills of loving is accepting that fact and keeping your relationships at peace.

Keeping peace with your mother does not mean you are not influenced by her anymore. Of course, you are influenced by your mother. Indeed, you are influenced by all your relationships. Nor does it mean you will let her run your life. Rather, it means you will not react to someone who reminds you of her as if that person were, in fact, your mother. You will not try to get something from others to make up for what your mother did not give you. You will take responsibility for living moment by moment rather than blame your problems on what she did to you. You will give up shouting no at her. You may never replace that no with a yes, but you will stop filling up your life with the no.

Making peace with someone does not mean that person will make peace back. Much as you might want that, you cannot force anyone to do what you want. Yet, you can be at peace with him or her, even though the person may be jumping up and down in anger at you. Of course, if you are attacked physically, you will duck. But you can duck in peace, as countless people who practice martial arts prove every day.

Making peace does not mean you have to like the person. You may dislike what he or she does intensely and still be at peace. You may not choose to spend time together. Robert Waterman suggested this silent blessing for such people: "I love you—God bless you—now please go away." Choosing to spent time with someone is totally different from choosing to make peace with that person.

Relationships consist of *selective memories and emotionally colored interpretations* of the past. Your relationship with your mother, for example, may be nothing like hers with you. It may have little to do with what happened physically between the two of you, since your memory may be inaccurate, limited to only a fraction of the events between you, or interpreted in unique ways. Relationships are not static; they change with each memory or interpretation. Yet, relationships have a convincing quality that makes you sure that your experience at this moment is the only one you could possibly have, given the circumstances of your life.

You have many relationships—with people, animals, objects, groups, events, your image of yourself, your image of God. You have relationships with what you see often, see rarely, see only in the past, or heard of and never saw.

If it is easy for you to keep your relationships peaceful, give thanks. Not everyone is so blessed. It may not be easy—it may take will, creativity, and patience—to use these practices to make and keep peace in your many different relationships. You may have to return to some practices often over time. If you can imagine what life will be like after you are at peace in all your relationships, even the most maddening, you will *know* the work is worth it.

Practice 61

DISCOVER YOUR HEARTFELT NOS

Love . . . keeps no record of wrongs.
ST. PAUL

In this practice you reflect on the many relationships you have developed throughout your life in order to locate those in which warring occurs. Some of your day-to-day relationships may be so negative that they come to mind at once. Thus you may not need to do this practice to discover subjects for future peacemaking.

Think through your life from when you were young to the present to see which relationships can pull you into them with an emotion-charged *no*. With whom do you get angry, scared, ashamed? In order to come up with more answers, head columns in your journal with the questions Who/What am I unwilling to forgive? and Who/What am I willing to forgive? Move back and forth between these questions, letting them trigger whatever responses emerge.

Look for leftover warring in each of your major relationships, such as those with parents, siblings, roommates, friends, employers, romantic partners, spouses, and children. With each such subject, head columns with What am I unwilling/willing to forgive (this person) for? For each person, develop a list of specific incidents that come to mind when you think of him or her. Identify the emotions that arise when you are drawn back into this relationship. Know whether your warring is directed at your subject, at yourself, or at both.

Practice 62
RANT AND RAVE

Only when you are fully able to say no will you become able to say yes! *from your whole being.*

WILLIAM ASHOKA ROSS

The purpose of this practice is to pick a warring relationship and dramatize to yourself your pain, bitterness, rage, condemnation, and feelings of superiority it evokes. Whenever various forms of *no* swirl through your life, use this practice to give them dramatice voice, safely, so you can get beyond them and learn from them. You cannot make peace by stuffing negative feelings off in a corner of your mind because you think you should not feel that way. By deliberately feeling the negative and exaggerating it, you begin to gain control over it.

Choose a relationship with which to do this practice. In your journal write an outrageously angry, damning, self-righteous condemnation of the person involved. Fully express your pain and all your negative judgments. Let everything out. Read over your writing several times, if possible out loud to a friend.

It is amazing what strong emotions you can feel as you do this. All these feelings are understandable, and you are not a bad person for having them. The question is whether you are willing to take control away from them and put it into your own hands, and do what it takes to make peace with the relationship.

The events are past. There is no way they can be undone. Yet the past does not cause wars—you are warring in the present, today. Your *no* today comes from the shortfall you see between what happened and what you think should have happened. Your interpretation of this shortfall injects the emotions: the judgment, good-bad, blame, shame, guilt, expectations (unmet demands, often in the form of shoulds, musts, and oughts), perfectionism, excuses, clinging, denying, right-wrong, catastrophizing (claiming that something is awful, horrible, terrible), win-lose, and dramatic agreement with friends and relatives.

There are three loving ways to get rid of the shortfall between your interpretation of the past and your demand.

1. Interpret the past more favorably to bring it up to your demand.
2. Lower your demand to meet the past.
3. Give up judging or making demands on what is past.

The rest of this chapter is devoted to practicing these ways. With these three methods, you can make peace with any event in your life, however violent and painful. Conversely, by hanging onto dramatic stories and high demands, you can make war with any events in your life, however nonviolent and painless.

Compassion

Compassion is the ability to see how it all is.
RAM DASS

Compassion is a way to interpret someone. With compassion you see the person's behavior against the broader plight in which he or she lives. Compassion departs from the world of good or bad people or good or bad deeds, the so-called realistic world that is taught by the media and reinforced in our everyday conversations. To be compassionate, you warm the way you interpret the incidents in your relationship and give up being locked into the cold, hard story as *the only true* story. This is so even if that story is obviously true, and everyone you know agrees with you that it is true.

An event never demands a particular meaning. Because meaning is the experience of relationship, you are free to create an event's meaning with any story that relates it to something else. If your husband once broke your confidence, this incident does not demand that you brand him as untrustworthy and thus a bad person. It does not mean that your relationship or your life is ruined because of the breach of trust. You could view him, for example, as a man who, like so many other men before him, let the little boy, inside get the better of his judgment in order to gain attention, approval, or pleasure. You could give up condemning him for his boyish qualities, some of which you might actually find delightful.

However negative your circumstances, there are compassionate viewpoints and stories, perhaps less dramatic, to tell about the same incidents. You do not have to give up your current interpretation. Just be willing to put others up alongside it, to take away some of its force and show there is a choice.

 ———————————————————————

Practice 63

VIEW THE OTHER PERSON WITH COMPASSION

If we could read the secret history of our enemies, we should find in each man's life sorrow and suffering enough to disarm all hostility.

HENRY WADSWORTH LONGFELLOW

Reflect on how your subject came to be the way he is or was. Think about his birth, his genes, his parents and family, and what it was like for him as a child. See him as a typical fallible, confused, struggling human—like you. Consider the society in which he was born and raised, his culture, his environment, the whole history that brought him into your life and made it natural for him to behave as he did.

See him in relation to *his* life, rather than yours. See

him as he saw himself. Describe some of the negatively charged events from his viewpoint. See his hopes and fears, securities and insecurities, blessings and handicaps, sensitivities and insensitivities, goals, joys, and sadnesses. Do the same for his parents and the other people important to him. See how the mistakes made by one generation of fallible people were passed on to the next generation, and so on until he came along.

Be sure to appreciate those qualities in him that you like. See that his behavior, however obnoxious, was fully human. We are all flawed, all succeeding and failing, striving and slacking off, always adding to the great statistical average that is humanity.

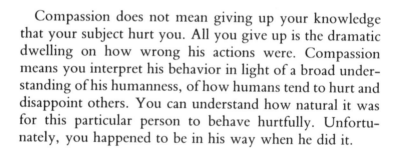

Compassion does not mean giving up your knowledge that your subject hurt you. All you give up is the dramatic dwelling on how wrong his actions were. Compassion means you interpret his behavior in light of a broad understanding of his humanness, of how humans tend to hurt and disappoint others. You can understand how natural it was for this particular person to behave hurtfully. Unfortunately, you happened to be in his way when he did it.

Practice 64

REWRITE THE OTHER PERSON'S STORY

Truth is that which works.
BUDDHA

This is a practice in compassion. You deliberately rewrite the story of one or more of the major incidents involving your subject. You change the circumstances from what *actually* happened to what might *ideally* have happened. Based on your compassion for her, you imagine her behaving in the best way possible, in a way that would have really worked, that would have caused what your compassion tells you she would have wanted if only she had been open and loving instead of closed and fearful.

If your subject is your parent, retell the incidents the way you wish you had been parented. Beneath the abuses, judgments, fears, and lies is the love that your parent wanted to share in the first place. Let her express that love now, in your imagination. Play with it, visualize it in its many details. Taste it, smell it, feel it, see it. Write it out in your journal.

Whenever the *actual* incident comes to mind, put your rewritten incident up alongside it. Have compassion for your subject's inability to create the ideal alternative. Dwell on the alternative instead of the *actual* event. Credit the person with good intentions, with wanting the loving alternative, but with having failed to find the way.

Practice 65

REWRITE YOUR OWN STORY

Experience everybody (or everything) in your life as either a teacher or a lover.

KEN KEYES, JR.

All events hold lessons if you actively look for them. Any time you encounter something you think you simply cannot love, that is a message to look for the lesson—one is in there somewhere.

This is a practice in compassion for yourself. Through it you can learn the lessons available in your relationships. Again, you imagine yourself in the same incident, only this time you respond, behave, think, and feel in the ways you now feel would have been best. If you were to go through the same experience again, only this time mature, self-confident, independent, and enlightened, how would you act? Put no limitations upon yourself; give yourself whatever abilities are called for. Go beyond merely wishing the experience away; do not say, for example, "The lesson I learned is never to trust men, so I wouldn't have been there with him in the first place." Instead, put yourself there, have him do what he did, but change the way *you* responded and record in your journal what you find.

Now, you will have at least three stories with which to interpret this incident—one in which you have re-written your story, one in which you rewrote the other person's story, and the original one that led to your being upset.

 ———————————————————————————

Challenge the logic in your usual story that keeps you in self-pity ("how unfairly I have suffered"), anger ("you should not have done that"), or depression ("I'm rotten and it is hopeless"). For example, you might be telling yourself, "It's unfair that I had parents as cruel as these." If so, respond with, "Of course it's unfair, but the world is unfair. Some kids will have winners for parents, some will have losers, and most kids will have ordinary parents." Having gone through your events with this person, having had lessons (perhaps hard ones) and having learned from them, what can you do now to have more compassion and love more deeply?

 ———————————————————————————

Practice 66

MAKE PEACE WITH THE DEMANDS OF OTHERS

Most human disturbance is a form of demandingness.

ALBERT ELLIS

Bringing peace to relationships means giving up making emotion-backed demands on others. Unfortunately, others do not give up making them on you. The world is full of demands, often masked as expectations—an expectation is just a wish plus a demand—some verbalized and some silent.

Parents get in the habit of making demands through their role of disciplining children and teaching them culture, and the children get in the habit of responding. Both habits carry into the rest of life, and people see it as quite appropriate to make demands on one another. Changing status from child to adult is tough on you and on your parents. Succeeding at *your* goals may mean losing at *theirs*. Compassion is called for on both sides, and you may be the only one capable of it.

You live in a world in which many people have wishes and demands for you. Make a list of all these people (dead or alive) and their specific expectations of which you are aware. Your goal is to make peace with each demand on your list, to see wishes and demands as part of the world, like rain and gravity. True, people can stop demanding, while gravity cannot turn itself off. But these people have not given up their expectations, and they show no signs of giving them up. They are part of your world, so you might as well calmly accept them. There is no need for you to demand that they stop making demands, though you may let them know that you are a free adult and can make your own decisions.

Sometimes, you will calmly make your own decision and not do what they want. You will have to view with compassion and perhaps sadness their unwillingness to admit that you are a free adult. You may have to watch peacefully while people you respect and love upset themselves needlessly about what you do, blaming you rather than their demands for their upset.

Sometimes, you will choose to do what they want. Indeed, their wishes might be what tips the balance in your decision. But whenever you go along with someone's demands, know well that the choice is yours. *You are not forced into it. You choose to do it.* Then and only then will you be able to stop the heartfelt no of resentment and struggle.

Forgiveness

Love is an act of endless forgiveness, a tender look which becomes a habit.

PETER USTINOV

To *forgive* means to make peace. You give up demands about how the past should have been, and thus you give up anger, resentment, and the desire or claim to punish. Forgiveness is not a matter of changing events. What happened, happened. Nor is it a matter of changing how you have interpreted events up to now. That too is in the past; it was the cause of the war you have been engaged in. Forgiveness means you shake off the past like dust, learn whatever it teaches, and get on with living. After all, you can appreciate the past, learn from it, or upset yourself about it, but you cannot change it.

Giving up demands about the past does not mean giving up asserting for the present and future. Asserting is not demanding; it is working to make sure that something you want to happen, happens. You can make peace with the fact that someone beat you up last week, while you resist and assert that he does not beat you up today.

Forgiving is not a bribe for improved behavior from your subject in the future. It is quite possible he will improve his behavior as you change how you feel and act toward him. But don't count on it.

Practice 67

DECIDE IF YOU ARE WILLING TO FORGIVE

It has been said that the continuation of the species is due to man being forgiving.

THE MAHABHARATA

Ask yourself if you are willing to bring peace to this relationship. Reflect carefully, perhaps in writing, before you answer, listing the pros and cons. Know that peace means giving up the dramatization of how right you are and how wrong the other person is. You will be giving up this excuse for suffering, for failing to achieve what you desire. You will be giving up this topic of conversation, this ever-present source of sympathy and support. But you also will be giving up the resentment around which your life revolves, which poisons this and other relationships, which keeps you from loving and learning as fully as this life permits. You will be asserting responsibility over making your life be as you would have it, not as a reaction to past circumstances.

Write out your answer as a statement of your intention: "I intend to do what it takes to forgive (this person)." The greater your determination to make peace, the sooner you will make it. Your statement of intention serves as a commitment to which you can refer and hang onto in the future should you ever become discouraged with your progress.

There's nothing wrong with being unwilling to make peace in a relationship. It may not be time yet. If you are not willing, then write out a statement in response to this question: When will the time be right for me to make peace with (this person)? Come back to this page from time to time and update it. Let it stand as a reminder that your loving path contains this heartfelt no that is waiting to be healed.

This is valuable in confronting your responsibility for warring relationships: You continue the war, not because the person was too obnoxious to make peace with, but because of a choice you made and keep making.

Practice 68

GIVE UP BEING RIGHT AND MAKING OTHERS WRONG

Would you rather be right or happy?
A COURSE IN MIRACLES

The language of right and wrong fuels war. Analyzing events along the right/wrong axis makes love impossible. "It was wrong of you to lie like that last night." "I was right when I yelled at Suzy." *Right* and *wrong* are pompous ways to label what you like and do not like so as to convince yourself and others that they are the preferences of God. By being aware, you can weed the right-wrong language out of your self-talk.

Watch your life for the next week and record each time you experience yourself as being right or wrong. Note the circumstances and what your internal voice is saying.

"This is right and that is wrong" is not the truth revealed from on high. It is just an internal voice—one among many. And *you* are not that voice; you are the person listening to it, capable of evaluating it according to your heart, capable of choosing to ignore it, give it further thought, or act on it. The more you listen to these righteous voices without taking them seriously, the more compassion you will have for all people, who live their lives with such confused and self-defeating chatter running in their minds.

Look inside to see if you get some pleasure out of condemning and feeling sorry for yourself, nursing your wounds. But isn't it a bitter and unsatisfying pleasure? Its cost is the turmoil of a relationship at war, and the person you really punish when you will not forgive is yourself.

Though your heart urges you toward forgiveness, you may hear a voice inside you saying that you should keep saying no because it serves him right. For the sake of justice, you should punish him. The fact that he did what he did in the past is so offensive in the present that you should keep shouting no. Calmly rebut this voice that cries for you to feel a kind of misplaced vengeance. Tell it there is nothing noble about making emotion-backed demands that the world be some way it obviously is not. By demanding, you just add your own war to a world that is already warring enough.

Finally, give up taking the right/wrong voices seriously —not because the person's behavior was not mistaken, but because you are determined to forgive. Internal voices cannot survive without your attention. When you hear the warring voice speak, turn your attention to other matters.

Practice 69

FORGIVE

Remember, you don't necessarily like their "act." You love the actors.

KEN KEYES, JR.

When you deny your "yes" because there is a shred of "no" left and you want to be absolutely sure that you have swept out all the darkness before you can claim your Light, I urge you not to be such a perfectionist.

EMMANUEL (PAT RODEGAST)

This practice is forgiveness—simply to let the past be in the past, and approach life in the present free from any nos from the past. Don't let the word *acceptance* get in your way. To accept the past does not mean you approve of it. It means simply that you do not fight with it.

Write a statement of forgiveness in your journal. Specifically include all the major negative events that come to mind. Assert, whether or not you feel like it, that you have given up all demands about how the past should have been, that you give up anger, resentment, and the desire or claim to punish. Include your understanding that forgiveness has nothing to do with the other person, but only to do with *your* judgments and demands. This statement is your choice, your commitment, your vision for guiding you in the future. While you may not always remember it or act according to it, it will always be there to pull you back onto your loving path.

Read your statement to others. That will give it more

reality. Ask them for support in helping you live up to your decision to forgive. That means that they will quietly remind you of your forgiveness when you seem to have forgotten.

If you find yourself accepting some past event intellectually but not emotionally, that means that you accept it once in a while. It implies the wish that you accepted it all the time. In order to do that, simply assert that you accept the past as past—once and for all. Should you find yourself drawn back once again into the familiar no of the relationship, immediately reassert that you simply *will not* indulge in warring. You control where you place your attention, and with practice you will get better at it.

Practice 70

LOOK FOR THE LOVE

My good father raged
*   When I snapped the peony—*
Precious memory!

TAIRO

The person you were at war with may have caused you great pain. Yet within this person lies a man or woman, boy or girl, wanting to love and be loved. Somewhere in you, most likely, is the ability to recall or create some love for him or her. After all, your love is probably the hook that keeps luring you back into your warring relationship. If you had no love, no positive feelings toward this person buried under the pain, you would likely have put the whole business out of your mind long ago. Yet the love is buried and, if it should peek out, you feel you should hide it from yourself so you can do justice to the negative feelings.

In this practice, deliberately look for affection, appreciation, caring, liking—as much as you can find, while you write in your journal.

You may have to look hard for features you can

appreciate and to put real effort into appreciating them. You may not find any. That is certainly all right. Perhaps later you will find some, perhaps not. Maybe the behavior that you disliked so much was the highest expression of love that person was able to come up with at that time. It is sad that people can be so blocked, but that is their plight; your life just happened to entangle theirs.

While doing this, you may uncover new areas of resentment, anger, or fear. If so, add them to the list in Practice 62, where you can work on them later.

❦ ———————————————————————— ❦

Practice 71

COMMUNICATE WHAT NEEDS TO BE SAID

A foolish consistency is the hobgoblin of little minds. . . . Speak what you think now in hard words and tomorrow speak what tomorrow thinks in hard words again, though it contradict everything you said today.

RALPH WALDO EMERSON

Often what keeps a relationship from peace is a communication you have never made: "I never told him I loved him." "I never thanked her." "I never said how much I resented it." "I never told her I wouldn't call her again." It is never too late to communicate if your goal is simply to make peace, to put the past responsibly behind you, and not to make your subject change his or her behavior. What you need to say to make peace may be at odds with what you have said before. All the more reason for saying it.

Just do it: face to face, by phone, by letter, by telepathy, any way you can. If the person is lost or dead, you still can do it. Express yourself in a letter, even if you cannot mail it. Or close your eyes, imagine the person with you, and talk.

With negative communications, first have a visualized conversation or one that you play-act with a friend. You can have your subject's image talk back to you, sometimes unpredictably. In the conversation, the person can hear your message and make peace with his or her side of the relationship. Thus you can express whatever you want, rehearse what you may say later in person, and go through great ranges of emotions—hate, anger, love, forgiveness, resentment, appreciation, or acknowledgment. Practice this; it works. If and when you finally have your negative communication in person with your subject, be gentle. Remember, this practice is a part of compassion and forgiveness, not permission to vent your anger.

Practice 72

CELEBRATE THE PEACEFUL RELATIONSHIP

Good, the more communicated, more abundant grows.

JOHN MILTON

When you make peace with a warring relationship, you often experience joy or gratitude for your subject, for yourself, for what you learned, or for the world. To fan even a tiny ember of such an experience into a blaze, celebrate it, enjoy it, revel in it, and communicate it to someone. Share the triumph of your now-peaceful relationship; let your subject or the world know how you feel.

Your purpose is solely to ratify your own celebration and add more love to the total of human conversation. Sharing something makes it real. If you love someone and tell that person or someone else, you usually love more richly. Even if the person responds by pushing you away with a defensive putdown, sharing has served your purpose.

Acknowledge how strong you have grown through your formerly warring, now peaceful, relationship, bad as it was at the time. Celebrate: "A toast to the role this person played in my life. Suffering through that relationship brought me where I am now. And I'm grateful."

Practice 73

KEEP YOUR RELATIONSHIPS AT PEACE

Love cures people—both the ones who give it and the ones who receive it.

KARL MENNINGER

And we must extinguish the candle, put out the light and relight it;
Forever must quench, forever relight the flame.

T. S. ELIOT

You can never make peace once and for all. You can make peace only for the moment, for now. It is a trap to think that once is enough—that because you worked so hard to feel at peace with your father yesterday, you should not hate him today. When you find yourself hating him today, the danger is in giving up and saying, "It's no use—I guess I'll always hate him. He's just hateful." Instead, you could say, "I did it yesterday, so it will be easier today, because now I've had practice."

Cultivate the habit of peace, so when someone acts in a way that used to trigger your heartfelt no, you're ready for it. You stay at peace, and you have a chance to love.

Take a stand that you love the people in your life. Then if, say, your child misbehaves, you never question the love. Your stand will displace the doubts that arise out of the misbehavior. Do not use inevitable negative circumstances to invalidate love. Loving often means asserting yes in the face of no from your friends and relatives. If you wait to love until your neighbors give approval, you may wait forever. Your neighbors are waiting for you to lead them. By loving you change your society, which in turn makes human nature more loving.

Each of your relationships is an invitation—to keep the peace, to grow, to learn, to change society, and to make a peaceful, loving planet. Do we, such small, lovely creatures, really know what ripples our tears of love bring across the universe?

The fingers and strings—they do not comprehend the ultimate reality of the music.

RABINDRANATH TAGORE

10 ❦ CRISIS LOVING

The diamond cannot be polished without friction, nor the man perfected without trials.

CHINESE PROVERB

One word frees us from all the weight and pain of life; that word is love.

SOPHOCLES

Every so often, life serves you a crisis—a disappointment, injury, illness, pain, or loss—that throws so strong a *no* into your face that it seems to close your heart. The practical consequences of these events are so unpleasant that only a heartfelt no seems possible. Yet closing your heart increases your suffering and leads to actions that contribute to a spiral of negativity in the world. Life, viewed as a training ground for loving, offers plenty of such crises as challenges to keep your heart open.

Sometimes crisis events are sudden and unexpected; at other times you can see them coming. Their inevitability often empowers the voice of fear, which dramatizes how bad the event is and projects an image of how much worse the future might be. On a path of loving, the challenge of life is to *un*empower the voice of fear and to use *all* the events of your life to love and to learn.

This chapter offers a set of practices for loving in crisis —steps you can take to get through a difficult time and stay on your loving path. It takes regular practice *before* a crisis to develop these skills so that they will be available to you when needed.

Practice 74

STOP FEEDING THE CRISIS

You cannot prevent the birds of sorrow from flying over your head, but you can prevent them from building nests in your hair.

CHINESE PROVERB

Crises are so dramatic and your internal voices are so compelling that you forget you can get offstage and witness what is happening from a seat in the audience. It may be days before you remember you could have done anything other than react according to script. The moment you notice you are in a crisis or approaching one, shout STOP! to yourself and get out of the drama and into the role of witness. To develop this skill, the practices in Chapter 7 are useful. As a witness, watch the actors, including yourself, and listen to their internal voices. Instead of reacting helplessly to the plot, you can choose how to respond.

If some familiar crisis recurs, prepare in advance for the events that trigger it. Post cards in conspicuous places around your home or office, reminding you to be prepared. Then when you see the crisis coming, immediately move out of the drama before it hits.

Practice 75

BREATHE DEEPLY

Becoming a Buddha by breathing is only a by-product of breathing. The most important purpose of breathing is to breathe and to enjoy breathing.

THICH NHAT HANH

In an upset or crisis you constrict your breathing. If you see a crisis coming or find you are in one, breathe deeply. With each out-breath, let out all the tension from your body and mind. By focusing on your breath you bring your attention away from the crisis to something positive and relaxing.

Practice 76

RELAX

When God gives hard bread, He gives sharp teeth.

GERMAN PROVERB

In a crisis you tighten your body. When you see a crisis coming or find you are in one, relax and move as gracefully as possible. Many methods exist for relaxing. One way is to go through your body systematically, first deliberately tightening a group of muscles as much as is comfortable, then letting go and relaxing as much as you can. You can use this practice at any time to develop a more relaxed feeling.

Practice 77

VISUALIZE FEELING PEACEFUL

What lies behind us and what lies before us are tiny matters compared to what lies within us.

RALPH WALDO EMERSON

In a crisis you war with the events in your life. So, when you are in crisis, deliberately feel at peace. One way to do that is to visualize yourself in some idyllic location, doing something that you associate with peace. Your breathing, relaxing, and visualizing will reinforce each other.

Practice 78

POSTPONE ACTION

Crises are the worst times for making decisions or taking important actions. When you are hurt, frightened, angry, depressed, and bombarded with unloving voices, do not act on them—let them be. Act later, when you are peaceful enough to be in touch with a full range of values and considerations. When action cannot wait, do nothing drastic. Take minimal actions that get you through to a time when you are poised again, able to think, feel, and choose clearly.

Practice 79

ATTEND TO WHAT IS HAPPENING NOW

Be here now.
RAM DASS

Spend the afternoon. You can't take it with you.
ANNIE DILLARD

Crises are fed by emotionally loaded memories of the past and projections into the future. So stop interpreting and stop projecting. Focus on what you are seeing, hearing, feeling right now. Whatever the crisis, there is something, the next step, waiting to be done. Just *do it* without agonizing over past and future. Chop wood, run around the block, love somebody. (Refer to the practices in Chapter 4.)

Practice 80

SPEAK POSITIVELY

Every morning and every evening, and whenever anything happens to you, keep on saying, "Thanks for everything. I have no complaint whatsoever."
SONO

Negative speaking, both out loud and inside your head, fuels crises. So replace it with positive expressions of joy or love. Even if your physical reality seems a disaster, you can force words of appreciation to drown out self-pity, fear, and anger.

Replace the negative voices in your head with a positive mantra. (Refer to Practice 47 on loving mantras.) Assert that the illness or trouble is a gift, a new beginning, a wake-up call, a challenge, or a new opportunity to love; then live up to your assertion. Make up a list of reasons why this experience will later seem to have led to your growth.

Practice 81

ACT THE PART OF A LOVER

Smiling is mouth yoga. . . . During a war, you see people dying; you see a lot of destruction around you. Smiling is one way to survive.

THICH NHAT HANH

Caught in a crisis, your feelings will not guide you in loving. When you want to be a certain way and do not know how, *act as if* you were that way. In crisis, even if you do not feel relaxed, *act* relaxed. Even if you do not feel loving, *act* loving. You will get so caught up in the role that loving will become real to you.

Practice 82

EXPLORE THE CRISIS WITHOUT WORDS

We hark to cricket
And to human chirpings—with
Ears so different.

WAFU

Your internal voices will interpret the events of your crisis in a barrage of words. In this practice, explore the crisis area in other, nonverbal ways—for example, with free, undirected drawings using pencil, pen, or colors. Make a number of these over a period of time. This acknowledges the crisis area and takes away some of its toxin. Also explore the issues in body movements, massage, or dance, or through drumming or other music-making.

Practice 83

LEARN WHAT YOU CAN

When we are no longer able to change a situation, we are challenged to change ourselves.

VIKTOR FRANKL

If you cannot love it, learn from it. Crises are excellent occasions for learning—dramatic enough to grab your attention, and tailored expressly for you.

Crises are often reactions to old events, triggered by something that harks back to those events. Describe carefully what it is that you fear, what upsets you. What, exactly, was the sequence of events that led up to the crisis, and how did you interpret those events?

For example, suppose you notice yourself slipping into a fight with your husband. Immediately shout STOP! to yourself and tell him you are not willing to go farther in this direction because you know where it will lead. Break the habit that leads to fighting.

Since the issue of your disagreement demands attention, dedicate a block of time for both of you to *learn*—about the issues, yourself, and each other. Start by acknowledging your love and respect for each other and for the relationship. Then, explore the facts regarding this issue. How does each of you interpret it? Who else is involved in it? What past events do you bring to the issue that color how you interpret it? In what ways do you see eye to eye on the issue and in what ways do you differ? Who can you ask to help?

If your husband is so caught up in the issue that he is not ready for a calm discussion, carry it out from your side anyway. When you are with him, dedicate yourself to learning about the issue. You perform a loving service to him, to you, and to the relationship by this practice.

Practice 84

MOVE YOUR SEAT BACK FROM THE STAGE

Man is not free from conditions. But he is free to take a stand in regard to them.

VIKTOR FRANKL

Events can become crises when you have no distance from which to witness them. In a crisis, move your seat back farther from the stage so that you broaden the perspective from which you look. Think of all the people you know, or all those who live in your city or state. What crises are they living with? Consider the billions of other people living on this planet and the crises in their lives. See Earth from space. View the sun and its planets as one of a hundred billion stars in the Milky Way, and view the Milky Way as one of perhaps a hundred billion galaxies in the universe.

Think of all the people who came before you in the countless years Earth has existed. Think of the life that will come after you. Even facing events that you do not like, can you feel grateful for being part of such an awe-inspiring world?

Practice 85

FEEL YOUR PAIN WITHOUT INTERPRETATIONS

All men suffer, now as well as in ancient times, but not all are unhappy, for unhappiness is a reaction to suffering, not suffering itself.

ALAN WATTS

Walk into your terror to learn its nature. It will be less painful if you do not turn away. Stay with the feeling itself, with no attempt to give it structure. It is structure that causes terror, not experience. You will see.

EMMANUEL (PAT RODEGAST)

In crises of sudden disappointment, loss, pain, illness, or injury, the voices in your mind immediately start interpreting the event, the other people involved, or yourself as awful, horrible, terrible, and unfair. Responding to these voices, you whip yourself into a negative froth of fear, anger, resentment, cynicism, depression, or futility. Depending on how strongly you hang on, a single crisis might throw you off your loving path for anywhere from moments to decades.

Your negative interpretations block any benefit the event might offer. You cannot, for example, learn what it is like simply to be without your boyfriend, because you are too busy telling yourself how lonely it is to be without him and how unattractive and worthless you must be because he left. You cannot experience simply working at your job, because you know how others must look down on you and how terrible it is not to have gotten the promotion. You cannot experience living with nausea and fever, because the disease you have is stated to be incurable.

When you are not consoled by the fact that people are always losing romantic partners, being passed over for promotions, and getting serious illnesses, you say that your life is too hard. Not just hard, which it clearly is, but *too* hard. The *too* means it is harder than you want and harder than you will stand, so you upset yourself and others about how difficult, unfair, and scary it is. Indeed, it is not fair. Life has never been fair. The hawk gets one bird and lets the other go. Thus it is—always.

In this practice, you put all labels and interpretations out of your mind and deliberately experience the practical results of your crisis fully. Live without your boyfriend and find out how it feels to cook and eat and spend the evenings by yourself or with other friends. Find out what it is like to go to work at your job without the promotion. Live life as deeply as you can while feeling nausea, chills, and fever.

Make a list of everything you now do or put up with that you think you should not have to endure. Whenever you think of something else that should not be the way it is, add it to the list. Ask yourself occasionally who, if not you, you think *should* have to do these things. Ask yourself what people, throughout the history of the world, have *not* had to put up with such conditions.

Practice 86

LAUGH IN THE FACE OF YOUR CRISIS

If you don't have a sense of humor, it isn't funny.
WAVY GRAVY

In order to see humor in anything, you must stand outside it in the position of witness. From that position, you create something uplifting out of the situation by seeing the incongruity and silliness in the plight of being human. You turn crisis into triumph by laughing in its face—not because the circumstances are funny, but with your conscious will, because you choose to.

Practice 87

SAY YES TO YOUR EXPERIENCE

So walk with your heaviness, saying "yes." Yes to the sadness. Yes to the whispered longing. Yes to the fear. YES.
EMMANUEL (PAT RODEGAST)

I accept the universe.
MARGARET FULLER

Resisting your crisis, shouting no at it, distracts your attention and saps your energy. Instead of no, shout yes—not because you like the situation, but as an assertion thrown into the world to give you a new standing place. Say "I love," and then live up to your assertion. Look around to see what there is to love. An immediate voice might say that nothing is left, but you know better. You love, simply because you give the word. This moment, this crisis, is showing you an aspect of human life, and you are doing what you can to love it.

Practice 88

MAKE THE LOVING CHOICE

Hold fear in one hand. Hold love in the other. Holding both, choose love and choose love again.

EMMANUEL (PAT RODEGAST)

In a crisis, too much seems to ride on the outcome of your choices. The intense story line in your drama makes it hard to reflect calmly about the consequences of various alternatives. Your sense of perspective is distorted, and your choices can easily reflect your anger, self-pity, or fear.

Even in a most dramatic crisis, however, you can step back and examine your alternatives. Do not ask which one you feel like choosing at the moment. You may not want to make the growth choice, the gracious choice, the forgiving choice. You may not want to take other people's feelings into account when you feel fear or pain. In crisis your feelings lose their value as guides. Ask, instead, *"What is the loving choice here?"* This may not settle the decision, as there are all kinds of love. But it will at least hold you on a path of loving and keep you from making choices that you will later regret, choices that add to a negative spiral.

Practice 89

REDIRECT YOUR ENERGY

My anger creates my verses.
QUINTILIANUS

Those who wish to sing always find a song.
SWEDISH PROVERB

Crises often rivet your attention onto yourself—on what you want or do not want, on what you are losing, on how inadequate you are. Put your attention off yourself and onto helping someone or doing something constructive. Get busy. You can redirect negative energy into related positive directions—such as anger to assertiveness, fear to alertness, sadness to caring. Write a poem or a letter. Many of the finest human actions throughout history have come from precisely this practice. Scrub the floor. If you are going to be in a crisis, your home might as well be clean.

Practice 90

TRANSFORM CRISIS INTO TRIUMPH

Love never fails.
ST. PAUL

Never despair. But if you do, work on in despair.
EDMUND BURKE

When life confronts you with an insurmountable opportunity, you can be crushed by it, or you can determine to turn it into a triumph. You may tremble in pain, loss, or fear, the way a leaf trembles in the wind. If so, *be* the leaf in the wind. That leaf is no coward, and neither are you. You are a human in the wind—it is human to tremble.

In this practice you turn your crisis into a triumph. What makes an event a triumph is not what you do or do not do, it is the attitude with which you do it. When you willfully confront your crisis and make of it the best you can, when you can say to yourself or others, "I am turning this crisis into a triumph," then you have indeed done just that. In particular, you turn crisis into triumph by choosing to experience the crisis—by really feeling the pain, the loss, or the fear.

You turn crisis into triumph by getting in touch with the deeper purpose of your desire that is being thwarted, and acting on that instead. If you wanted

Christmas to be a time of love and sharing with your children and they will not be able to visit you this Christmas, celebrate the holiday as a time of love and sharing with others.

You turn crisis into triumph by making peace with the past, being accepting enough that you can finally leave the past as truly past. As *no* binds you to the past, *yes* frees you to love today.

You turn crisis into triumph by learning as much as you can, however strongly you dislike the events. Tell yourself, "I can learn and grow from this crisis. There is something to learn here—what is it?"

Most major crises involve loss. Thus, the next chapter is devoted to the challenge that losses pose to your ability to love.

How strange that so often it all seems worth it.
                                        SHELDON KOPP

11 ❦ LOVING THROUGH LOSS

The clouds pass and the rain does its work,
and all individual beings flow into their forms.

I CHING

This too shall pass away.

ANONYMOUS

Whatever comes will go. You confirm that truth over and over, with big things and small. Whoever you are with will depart, or you will beat them to it. Whatever you are doing will end, or you will no longer be around to do it. When you are young, healthy, and upbeat, you can forget this truth, but not for long. Soon you lose something you value. You take down the Christmas tree and go back to school. Your dog gets hit by a car. You move to another grade or another town. You have to start wearing glasses. Your parents divorce.

Slowly your thoughts fill with wonderful memories. It hits home that this too—whatever *this* may be—really shall pass away. You can imagine a future, as certain to arrive as the present moment was, when you are no longer able to play ball, or take care of your home, or walk, or even get out of bed.

You start life by losing the womb. Then, in changing from baby to child, you lose closeness with your mother. As brothers and sisters join and leave your family, you lose familiar roles. You lose childhood and adolescence, innocence and virginity. The romance you desperately want to work out often does not. You lose the childless state by having children and lose the role of parent when your kids grow up. You lose the single state through marriage and the married state through death or divorce. Loved ones die, even the ones you love the most, the ones with whom you have shared everything. You may lose dreams, trust, self-esteem, jobs, success, money, skills, purpose, meaning, optimism, and idealism. The face in the mirror gets ever older. Eventually you begin to lose control—over your body, your income, your sense of independence, your home, and your confidence that this life will keep going on. And what is the alternative to losing a lot of things slowly, one after another? Losing a lot of them quickly!

Each loss leaves a hole. There is no point pretending it does not. Some of the holes are large. And still life goes on, always with the challenge to use the crisis produced by the loss to experience deeply how mysterious it all is, and, when appropriate, to get up once more and love.

Practice 91

COUNT YOUR LOSSES

Perpetual giving up is the truth of life.
RABINDRANATH TAGORE

Head a page in your journal, Losses I Have Had. Then think back over your life and write down the losses that come to mind—people, animals, objects, abilities, security, environments, possessions, jobs, anything you recall when you read the page heading. As you recall an item, let yourself vividly experience memories of your relationship with it.

Then, head another page, Losses I Will Have, and imagine losses you may well have throughout the rest of your life. Write them down, in a likely order, imagining what they might be like—all the way to your death.

Note which of these many losses, past and future, you are not at peace with, which ones keep pulling you to remember or imagine them with a heartfelt no.

Practice 92

**ACKNOWLEDGE YOUR SKILLS AT COPING
WITH LOSS**

In this practice you realize how many skills you have
already acquired for coping with loss. Go through your
list of past losses from Practice 91 and for each one
write down what you did to cope. What coping skills
did you strengthen by going through this experience?
Some skills that people commonly discover are faith
(in God, in things getting better, in themselves or other
people, in future growth); replacement (getting a new
cat, finding a new romantic partner); knowing others
go through loss; loving other people, animals, and activities; talking; crying; shouting; distractions (buying
things, working hard, socializing, sex); exercise (hit-
ting a punching bag, sports, running); work; humor;
sleep; indulgence; time; creative or artistic expression;
writing; making or listening to music; and reverently
keeping the memory alive. Some of the ways you may
have coped with loss, like denial or addiction, might
have multiplied your troubles. In that case, you have
learned habits to avoid in the future.

Steps to Loving Through Loss

> *Through love, sickness is health,*
> *Through love, wrath is as mercy.*
> *Through love, the dead rise to life.*
> THE MASNAVI I MA'NAVI

Besides the steps for loving in crises given in Chapter 10,
here are some specific steps you can take to pave the way
for loving in times of loss.

Practice 93

DON'T MAKE MORE LOSSES

One loss is enough, so be careful about creating more. It is easy to say, "What difference does it make? Things are already as bad as they can get!" But, no matter how bad things are now, they *could* get worse.

Beware of conclusions or decisions made in the pain of loss: "I'll never trust another man." "I can never succeed in this profession." "I will never get married." Such decisions often bury themselves deep in your soul and show up later to sabotage a relationship or lead you to make a disastrous professional decision.

Also, as discussed with Practice 78 on postponing action in time of crisis, beware of taking quick actions in time of loss that might later look like mistakes. For example, during the pain of deep loss, it is a poor time to break off ties with someone, quit a job, or sell your house and move to an apartment.

Practice 94

MAKE PEACE WITH THE RELATIONSHIP

Often, your pain over a loss is complicated by the fact that your relationship with the subject is filled with negative memories. "I hated my father for being an alcoholic, and now that he has died I will never be able to let him know I loved him." The time of a loss, actual or envisioned, is the perfect time to do whatever it takes to make peace with this relationship. Chapter 9 is devoted to making peace with relationships. You can also use its practices in the context of loss.

Pain is perhaps the toughest area of human life to accept, and people have used it to forge the most triumphant, as well as the most degrading, experiences imaginable.

You may agonize over the pain being experienced by the people caught up in the loss, but agonizing over someone else's pain is not likely to stop it. All you can do is play it over and over again in your mind. Are you willing to stop that and let your subject's pain become part of the world, part of a long history that holds much pain, without adding your own to the total?

There is a difference between sensitivity and vulnerability. Sensitivity means being as aware as possible, and awareness is a form of loving. Through awareness you deepen your experience. Sensitivity permits you to respond to this person, animal, or situation in the most supportive, useful way.

On the other hand, vulnerability means reacting to someone else's pain by adding your own to it. If you are vulnerable, it may be that seeing another in pain or confronting someone's death makes you confront the fact that *your* life is bound to contain pain and *you* are bound to die. If so, admit that you are agonizing not for the other person, but for yourself.

 ——————————————————————————

Practice 95

STOP FIGHTING OTHER PEOPLE'S PAIN

O God, Creator of mankind, I do not aspire to comprehend You or Your creation, nor to understand pain or suffering. I aspire only to relieve the pain and suffering of others, and I trust in doing so, I may understand more clearly Your nature.

ST. FRANCIS OF ASSISI

In this practice you stop creating pain for yourself because of vulnerability to the pain of others. Your aim is to be sensitive to the other person's pain but not to make an emotion-backed demand that it stop. As you are able to do that, you give the other an environment in which to experience pain for herself, without having to feel responsible for the feelings of the people around her. This lets her minimize her own pain and maximize her growth. It also permits you to stay open and present with those who are suffering, rather than burn out or run away physically or emotionally because you hurt too much to be with them.

Make a list of the pain of others, past or present, that you fight against. Listen to the internal voice demanding that this pain not exist, and write out what it says. Distinguish between loving other people and upsetting yourself by demanding that they not suffer. (To increase your sensitivity and intimacy with your subject, you can use the practices in Chapter 8. In order to keep from being sucked into vulnerability, you can use the practices of Chapter 7.)

Practice 96

MAKE PEACE WITH THE MEANING OF THE LOSS

The ocean does not shrink or vaster grow,
Though the waves ever ebb and ever flow;
The being of the world's a wave, it lasts
One moment, and the next it has to go.
NARUDDIN ABDUR RAHMAN JAMI

So often a loss just does not make sense to us. The promise or expectation that will go unfulfilled because of it dramatizes its irrationality. Write out the most important meanings you see in the loss you confront. "How tragic that she was never able to finish her book. The world would have been so blessed by it." "He was such a good father, and now his children will have to go on without him."

Now, acknowledge the truth of the loss. It certainly would have been better if the author could have finished her book, or if the father could have lived to continue parenting. However, you could focus on what the person did accomplish. For each "If only . . ." statement, write out some "How wonderful that . . ." statements. Change from dwelling on the tragedy of what your subject did not have a chance to do, to dwelling on the triumph of what the person did accomplish.

Practice 97

LOVE THROUGH GRIEVING

What soap is for the body, tears are for the soul.

JEWISH PROVERB

Grieving is an experience of deep love under the particular illumination of loss. It uses the dramatic circumstances of the loss to intensify loving feelings, thoughts, and actions. Yet it is easy to miss the *yes* you are directing toward your loved one under these circumstances because of the pain of the powerful *no* you direct toward the fact of his or her departure.

Experience as fully as you can all the diverse and often contradictory reactions stimulated by the loss. These might be memories, voices in your mind, feelings, wishes, frustrations, judgments, anger, hurt, loneliness, fear, sorrow, pain, love, relief, joy, confusion, completion, despair, pride, ache, hilarity, freedom, guilt, satisfaction, martyrdom, emptiness, betrayal, amazement, gratitude, and "why me?"

The time of loss is the time to unearth and experience *all* the elements of your relationship with your subject. To evoke these experiences, write them out in your journal, tell them to a friend, or visualize your subject and speak them to him. Know that it is perfectly natural to have contradictory feelings about a loved one: You may be furious with him for having left you, at the same time in deepest sorrow at his loss.

Use the occasion of loss to deepen your love. To do that, interpret your pain not so much as a *no* toward the loss as a profound *yes* for your loved one. Make your grieving a conscious strengthening of your bonds of love.

Now, with the loss fresh in your mind, your grieving is most intense. As its intensity lessens with time, you will notice that you spend less time fighting the fact of the loss and move on to loving the rest of your life and your memories of your beloved.

Practice 98

EXPRESS THANKS TO YOUR LOST BLESSING

What is the poetic nature? Things mean; they mean deeply; they mean infinitely.

R. H. BLYTH

This practice is widely used for deepening love in the grieving process and for making peace with painful loss. It helps you to turn pain into a triumph of spirit over circumstances. In this case, you turn loss, even the most profound, into creation—a piece of writing or a work of art.

Deliberately use your sense of loss to heighten your awareness of how intensely you love and have loved your subject. As you cultivate that awareness, turn it into a piece of writing, prose or poetry, in which you express your heartfelt thanks to your subject for being such a blessing to you. Besides writing, you may play or sing music, dance, paint, or draw. Express your most poignant memories and the depth of your feelings. You may want to show the resulting creation to others, but it is enough to use the creative process to evoke the experience and the experience to evoke the creating.

This practice consciously builds up a heightened sense of love and gratitude for your subject when you think about the loss. Keep holding up a thank-you as you approach your subject, and soon your gratitude and loss will begin to merge. As you grow used to thanking the universe for its generosity, it will become easier for you to *trust* it with your future.

This practice helps you let in the truth of what you have lost, rather than live in denial. In denial you try to protect yourself from pain by sticking your knowledge of the loss into one corner of your mind and walling yourself off from awareness of it. This blocks the love in your relationship and keeps you from living at peace. Your energy is constantly drawn to protecting the wall, lest you see the truth through it. Denial is an extreme form of evasion, in which you scream so loud a no at the loss that you dare not look at it. Temporary use of evasion may actually work well for you by feeding your awareness with truth at a rate slow enough for you to cope with.

The loss of a beloved is negative enough without your fighting it forever. There is no pat answer to the question of how soon your no will fade away and leave you with the yes of your love. Many factors might urge you to keep fighting a loss. The pain may be just too great to do anything else. Life might have more meaning when you are caught up in a dramatic tragedy. You might think that accepting the loss without anguish would prove that you did not love. The people around you also might expect you to dramatize your loss, and they might give you special attention and care because you have lost so much.

Perhaps the greatest testimony you can make to your love for someone is to live as lovingly as possible after that person is gone. You can ask openly for the attention and care you want, rather than suffering such anguish that people feel moved to give it to you. Perhaps, if you continue leading a positive life in spite of your loss, you will inspire the people around you to do the same.

Practice 99

STOP FIGHTING THE LOSS

The deepest question (that the world puts to us) admits of no reply but the dumb turning of the will and tightening of our heartstrings as we say, "Yes, I will even have it so!"

HENRY JAMES

Self–surrender is synonymous with eternal happiness.
                                    SRI RAMANA MAHARSHI

Head a page in your journal Am I Willing to Stop Fighting This Loss? Then explore in writing the many voices that come to mind in answer. Challenge the truth of the voices that say no. Since everyone loses beloved people, objects, and abilities, why should you be spared? Why should your preferences be made into the rules governing the world?

Loss, especially other people's loss, is easy to *think* about handling. At one extreme, you can make it trivial: "So my husband died—so what's the big deal? Lots of husbands die. Don't overdramatize it." This approach may tempt you because, after all, your goal is to lessen the drama and make peace with the loss. Yet no one wants to trivialize one of the most powerful experiences of life. At the other extreme, you can wallow in the loss: "How terrible that my husband died. How I must grieve, suffer, live in the past now that he is gone forever." This approach plays into a love of drama.

Clearly, neither of these approaches fits. And yet, both of them fit. Your husband's life *is* now in the past. Your love for him is secure, and there *are* lots of things in your life you can love. You would be wise to get on with loving them, sooner or later.

Your husband's presence was wonderful. You entwined your life with his. Now that he is gone, your life is changed permanently. Some of what you previously used to give it meaning and joy lives now only in memory. It is by finding new ways to create meaning, new things to love, that you will find that living seems worthwhile again. This requires changing from the old ways. You need to let go of what was, let go of what was not, and let go of what might have been. That means letting the wonderful past be wonderful without clinging to it. It means not agonizing about all those events that would have been so wonderful, but that never happened. Life is now, and love is now.

Practice 100

LEARN WHAT YOU CAN

Nothing in life is to be feared. It is only to be understood.

MARIE CURIE

There is only one teacher—life itself.

CHARLOTTE JOKO BECK

Whatever you are going through, even if there seems to be nothing you can love in the experience, there is bound to be something you can learn. In this practice, you look into the loss and your reaction to it to explore what you can learn from it, how you can grow from it.

You might find you can learn compassion, for yourself and others, by pondering the suffering of all the people who have lived. You can feel at one with the pain, loss, and helplessness of countless people from the past and present, and thus you feel akin to the whole stream of life.

You might learn how attached you are to people, abilities, and objects. This gives you a chance to let go of what you were clinging to, what you thought you *had* to have. You may learn to confront death and develop a philosophy of life.

Loss can teach you what you value. It puts you in touch with what you are doing with your life. It teaches you how to use your time, to go for the rich and meaningful and leave the superficial alone. It urges you to increase the power of your will—to achieve what you determine to achieve.

When loss brings fear and sorrow, you may learn you can make it through tough times. Loss can teach you to depend on yourself rather than on what is outside you. It teaches you respect for the objects you love and for the people who support you in troubled times. It also teaches that new doors always open as old ones close.

Practice 101

TRANSFORM LOSS INTO TRIUMPH

When the heart weeps for what it has lost, the spirit laughs for what it has found.

SUFI SAYING

Sometimes when loss overwhelms you, there seems to be no meaning in anything you do or give to the world or in any of the experiences of loving. At such a time, you may simply have to bow your head before the great mystery that gives and takes away.

Even then, there is a way to show your love of the world and life: by the *stand* you take toward your suffering and loss. When life challenges you in these strongest terms, accept that you feel no love. Feel your pain fully, deliberately. Experience your despair as deeply as you can.

Then choose the attitude you will take toward the world despite your misery. Adopt a stance of courtesy, courage, cheer, and loving actions. Thereby you give meaning to your loss and to your pain. Pain and loss are the sandpaper by which life will fashion you into a work of art. Have compassion for yourself for suffering so deeply. In so doing, you are walking your loving path.

Using the Certainty of Loss to Deepen Your Love

Without the awareness of death he would be an ordinary man involved in ordinary acts. He would lack the necessary potency, the necessary concentration that transforms one's ordinary time on earth into magical power.

DON JUAN (CARLOS CASTANEDA)

By reflecting on the certainty of loss, you can deepen your loving. When you deny that loss is certain, you take for granted whatever is in your life. No need to pay attention to it—after all, there are endless tomorrows. But if you accept, truly accept, that everything is temporary, you are moved to love whatever you touch while you touch it. It will soon be gone.

If you hug your daughter while reflecting on loss, you will feel her and pour love into her. She will not be there long. When the hug is over, you can let her go to bed without hanging onto her. This time she is just going to bed. A later departure will be more dramatic, in a form you cannot now predict. Nevertheless, her ultimate departure from you is inevitable. That is the inevitability of the loss of every blessing in your life. Clinging seems foolish. You can let her go—this time, to bed. Next time, to what?

Each time you let go of anyone or anything, release it to the universe, grateful for having shared life and energy with it.

The very word *loss* suggests that you own or control something before it is taken away. Yet, you own nothing and no one—no person, animal, plant, object, sense, or ability. You just get to share life with them, take care of them, in some cases make use of them, for a while. You are their steward, blessed to have them with you for a while to love and learn from. Even your body you do not own, but instead you animate and care for it. The view of ownership comes from fear, not love. If what you love seems scarce, you will fear its loss, and the fear creates the clinging and controlling of ownership. Practice 45 is useful for exploring the role of ownership in your life.

View your blessings as either things to care for or to care with. When one is taken from you, your question becomes, What will I care for now? or What will I care with now? You can transform the saying, "Every ending is a new beginning," from a tired cliché into the approach you take to endings.

You need not make a problem out of dying, something to be worried over and fussed about. That would be as if a plum, ripening on a tree, thinks how horrible it will be to fall off. Dying is no problem—it takes care of itself. You do not have to do anything to die. It is only living that offers you a challenge. However pained or ill you may be, you have only to live on your path of loving—just this moment—just now.

Practice 102

COUNT YOUR BLESSINGS

It is permissible to take life's blessings with both hands, provided you know that you are prepared in the opposite event to take them just as gladly. This applies to food and friends and relatives, to anything God gives and takes away.

MEISTER ECKHART

Head pages in your journal Blessings I Have Had, and Blessings I Will Have, and make lists in the same way you did in Practice 91, "Count Your Losses." Again, take a moment to remember or imagine specific loving events.

When you have finished, go back and make sure that you have included on your lists of blessings every item that was on your list of losses in Practice 91. After all, in order for the absence of something to strike you as a loss, its presence must have been a blessing to you in the first place.

This and Practice 91 illuminate the natural events of your life in two ways. Looking at losses focuses on the fact that blessings inevitably leave, while looking at blessings focuses on the fact that blessings inevitably come. Events never require you to focus one way or the other. You are free to choose what the events of your life will mean—a shower of blessings or a runoff of losses.

In time of loss, you focus on the difference between what is now present and what used to be present. That difference is often enormous. No words can express the difference between the presence and absence of a beloved in your life. The mystery of loss dramatizes the mystery of presence. "Was it only a minute (month, decade) ago that she stood before me, vital and alive? And now she is gone—that laugh and joy and wonderful energy are gone!"

You do not and never will really *understand* how any person, animal, plant, object, or ability has come into being out of the stuff of the universe. While you are blessed with it, you are free to love it. Once it is gone, you are free to love its memory. But of one thing you can be sure: The lovable will always come, in one form or another, and you will always have the power to love it. You have a surplus of lovable people and objects in your life—always—if you but look around. No matter how much you lost or how recently you lost it, what you have left is more than enough to appreciate.

Practice 103

THANK YOUR CURRENT BLESSINGS

i thank You God for this amazing
day: for the leaping greenly spirits of trees
and a blue true dream of sky; and for everything
which is natural which is infinite which is yes

E. E. CUMMINGS

I am dancing, dancing earnestly to the Great Spirit,
And dance and dance til I can dance no more.

POTAWATOMI CHANT

Pick one of the current blessings from your list from Practice 102 and express thanks to it in the same way you did to your lost blessing in Practice 98. Imagine having lost it in order to open up words, music, art, or dance that calls out deeper love, which in turn calls out more expressive action. Express your deepest thanks to your subject for being such a blessing in your life. If your subject is a person and it is appropriate to do so, share your writing with her. She will be touched by knowing how much she means to you.

 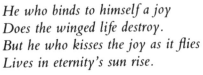

He who binds to himself a joy
Does the winged life destroy.
But he who kisses the joy as it flies
Lives in eternity's sun rise.

WILLIAM BLAKE

12 ❧ LOVING THROUGH ACTION

It's not how much you do, but how much love you put into the action.

MOTHER TERESA

A ctions both express and evoke experience. Behavior reinforces the attitude behind it. So in order to be more loving, you can put more *yes* into either what you do or what you experience. Either way, the *yes* enters into the cycle of reinforcement between your private experience and your public behavior. Because people tend to become like those around them, as you express more love, the people around you become more loving. Thus your private acts of loving multiply and ripple around the world.

Practice 104

HOW DOES THIS ACTION EXPRESS LOVE?

*Every stroke of my brush
Is the overflow
Of my inmost heart.*

SENGAI

This practice is the systematic interpretation of all your frequent activities as expressions of loving (see Practice 22). That does not mean that your roles do not express other purposes as well: earning a living or associating with other people, for example. When you play a role while willfully using it to express loving, your experience intensifies the love you are expressing.

Head a journal page, What Are My Major Roles in

Life? List as many as you can, and for each role, list the major actions that you frequently take. Describe each role and action as vehicles for loving. How is doing this an expression of your love? For example, you can mow the lawn as a celebration of contact with the earth, of growth, life, and beauty, as service to your family, neighbors, and community. When you have worked out this list, be aware of the many ways your actions express your love when you do them in the future.

❧ ——————————————————————————— ❧

Practice 105

REASONS I DON'T LOVE DOING THIS

We die on the day when our lives cease to be illuminated by the steady radiance, renewed daily, of a wonder, the source of which is beyond reason.

DAG HAMMARSKJÖLD

In this practice you confront what you dislike about your activities. Head a journal page, What Do I Do That I Don't Love Doing? This will highlight tasks that are especially ripe for this work.

Pick a single task and head a page, I Don't Love Doing X Because _____. List as many reasons as come to mind. Notice how solid and objective these reasons seem. For example, you could not possibly love your work if it involves standing and your feet hurt.

Ask yourself if you are *willing* to delight in this work, despite the apparent truth of your reasons. Even though your feet hurt, are you willing to delight in waiting on customers? If so, whenever you do this task, stay in touch with your purpose. Say to yourself, "This (customer, task, employer) is a mirror—it reflects back my state of mind, my focus on either the negative or the positive." This will confuse the voices that chant your reasons for disliking the activity. Thus, while your reasons for disliking the task may be valid, you give them less power.

Practice 106

ACT FROM AN IMAGE OF YOURSELF AS LOVER

Nothing being more important than anything else, a man of knowledge chooses any act, and acts it out as if it matters to him.

DON JUAN (CARLOS CASTANEDA)

In this practice, you construct a mental image of yourself in your common activities as that of a lover. First, for the many activities on your lists from Practices 104 and 105 ask, What image do I have of myself in this role? The image may be expressed by pictures or an internal voice saying, for example, that when you buy groceries you are working as a servant to an ungrateful family that wants not only better meals but also less money spent on groceries.

Next, rehearse in your imagination how a person would play this role, do this action, while in the deepest love. How would Mother Teresa buy groceries? Project these images on your mental screen, and watch and feel yourself behave this way. Then, as you perform the action, first create the mental image of yourself as a lover, and then act out that image. *Be* Mother Teresa buying groceries.

Do not worry that *acting as if* differs from *the real thing*. The experiences are similar—just ask an actress who has been playing a love scene. Your previous acting out of habit, as if your behavior had nothing to do with loving, also evoked feelings—of cynically going through the motions—and it was no more the real thing than this. Make the real thing be a loving life. Settle for nothing less.

Practice 107

WHAT IS THE PURPOSE OF THIS ACTION?

It is the consistent choice of the path with heart which makes the warrior different from the average man. He knows that a path has heart when he is one with it, when he experiences a great peace and pleasure traversing its length.

DON JUAN (CARLOS CASTANEDA)

Society tends to see getting something done as the purpose of most actions. That is reasonable, since society recently emerged from a condition of poverty in which people often had to get the job done in order to survive. If they failed, cold, hunger, and disease awaited them. These days, your physical survival does not hang on whether you get the next promotion or how clean your kitchen is, yet you may still be bringing survival motivation to your actions. Working at your job in order to achieve the symbols of a promotion is far different from working at your job as a vehicle for loving.

If you do something just to get it done, when you are finished your experience will be of having done one more task. If you do something as a means to express your love, your experience will be of caressing the world as you do it. Actions are means to the heartwarming experiences of loving as well as means to reaching a goal.

Whatever you are doing, ask yourself, "To what purpose am I committed?" You may find the answer to be "none, I'm doing it because I have to," "to reach this goal," "to earn some money," "to please someone," "to have something to occupy my time," or "to convince myself that I am worthwhile."

Loving actions begin not with technique but with loving. So assert that you are using your actions to express a particular loving purpose. This purpose might be the welfare of another, a group, an enterprise, posterity, or the world. It might be to make something function according to your values, or to do something efficiently, or communicate something, or express a feeling, create intimacy, cooperate, make something beautiful, find a truth, learn a lesson, make a world in which conflicts are settled peacefully, or to live so that generations to come will be able to have richer lives.

Practice 108

USE THIS ACTION TO EXPRESS CARING

Caring is the greatest thing, caring matters most.
FRIEDRICH VON HÜGEL (LAST WORDS)

All motives boil down to caring. All actions reflect what you care for most at this moment. Whenever you choose to do something, you choose what you are going to care for. The challenge of a loving path is to care ever more intensely about whatever is present in your life, while not getting attached to the way the circumstances work out. You can pour care into the world, but if you demand that your activities turn out the way you want, you hook yourself on something you cannot control.

Here you apply the deliberate cultivation of mindfulness, Practice 27, to make your actions expressions of your loving. Before you undertake an action, pause, and then commit to using the action to express your caring. Then care—care deeply, and through the activity caress the world. Relax physically and move gracefully. Caress the piano when you play it, and let the sound caress the world. Your mantra: "With this act I caress the world."

Practice 109

ENGAGE WHOLEHEARTEDLY IN WHAT YOU ARE DOING

Somebody's boring me—I think it's me.
DYLAN THOMAS

At the funeral of a great Hassidic master, a disciple was asked what was most important to his master. He responded, "Whatever he happened to be doing at the moment."

HASSIDIC STORY

Bored, dull, burned out, going through the motions —these are the experiences of our time. If love is a heartfelt yes, you may have long ago decided love was not for you, because how long has it been since you experienced a heartfelt anything?

First you feel bored, so you blame your feeling on a world that is not interesting enough. Since nothing stimulates you enough for you to want to engage in it, you withdraw into inactivity and your will runs down and grows flabby with disuse. Your lack of engagement in life snowballs.

In this practice you engage yourself, wholeheartedly, in whatever you may be doing. Head pages in your journal, What Do I Do That's Not Worth Doing? Keep notes during a week or two. Look into yourself to see what makes something worth doing or not worth doing. Why are you doing something that is not worth doing—why not just stop? If you have valid considerations for continuing it, then isn't the action worth doing after all?

When you know clearly what the payoff is for doing those things on your list, ask whether you are going to continue using your time to do them. If so, then ask if you are willing to engage in doing them wholeheartedly. Are you willing to be moved by doing them? If so, then stop evaluating them, stop judging them, stop fighting them—*engage* in them.

The source of interest is engagement; the source of enthusiasm is participation. Allocate enough time for whatever is at hand. Animate your engagement— broaden your hand gestures and facial expressions, talk louder, higher, and lower. Determine to pour your whole attention and care into life.

Practice 110

LET THE PARTICULAR STAND FOR
THE GENERAL

Inasmuch as you have done it unto the least person among you, you have done it unto me.

JESUS

In this life, I didn't get to put all the world's children to bed. I got to put Karen and Elizabeth to bed. Just them. Yet so many nights at bedtime, the voice in my mind would say, "I don't want to stop reading or writing just to get up and put you to bed." There is Elizabeth—the familiar, the usual, the one who is always there at this hour. "I've done this before." Yet if I want to hug a child—to touch her with love and read to her and put her to bed—this is my chance, my only chance. Through you, Elizabeth, I can express how much I love children—maybe a billion of them in the world—some beautiful, some hungry, some frightened, some lonely, and some happy. Only as I laugh with you and touch you do I laugh with and touch all children.

Let the particular people, objects, or tasks before you stand as offerings from the universe for you to love. They stand for all people, objects, and tasks. Do not refuse to love these particulars because you are waiting for life to offer you something so powerful you will *have* to respond to it. When you serve another, experience serving humanity. *You* have responded to *this person*. You have helped *this* man solve his problem. You have made *this* woman laugh. You are not just following a formula for service and trusting it to get you through the day.

Let the particular person, object, or activity—the one that is before you now—stand for the general. Express your love for all people through this particular person you are talking with, your love for the entire earth through this particular flower you are watering. You can make love to the universe only through those personifications of the universe that come into your life.

Working Toward Your Own "Bottom Line"

Work is love made visible.
KAHLIL GIBRAN

In the workplace and media you hear a lot about "the bottom line," meaning an agreed-upon measure of value of the ultimate output of an activity. Your job may have its official bottom line—greater production, greater profits, greater market share, more clients served, higher pay. But measures of the bottom line omit the *heart* of the activity, which is the love of the people involved in it.

When you stop attending to loving, for whatever reasons, you are on the path to burnout. You can burn out from any part of life—from your job, your marriage, parenthood, a hobby, your pet, or your favorite entertainment—or from all of it. If you pay attention to loving whatever you are doing, then you will not burn out, you will burn with the fire of an ever deeper love. Any practice that deepens loving will keep you from burnout. Here are a few that keep you working toward your own bottom line, toward loving life through work.

Practice 111

BE CLEAR ABOUT YOUR "BOTTOM LINE"

What does it profit a person to gain the whole world and lose his soul?

JESUS

Regardless of the official bottom line for any action you take, be clear about *your own*. Know that all actions are ultimately excuses for loving. Fortunately, some actions bring added benefits like production and pay, which in turn can contribute to human joy as these benefits ripple throughout the world.

While acknowledging benefits like production and pay, hold to your own bottom line, the ultimate purpose of your activity, which is to pour loving energy into the world—to contribute to the lives of your fellow workers and your clients and customers, to offer what the world needs, to give you a vehicle for service. It takes determination and practice to work toward your own bottom line when those around you seem to have bought an official one. That determination and practice is part of a path of loving. It will, in time, transform the world.

Practice 112

DELIGHT IN THE WORK, NOT THE APPLAUSE

All for love, and nothing for reward.
EDMUND SPENSER

It is not necessary to have great things to do. I turn my little omelet in the pan for the love of God.
BROTHER LAWRENCE

Serve others for the joy of service, rather than to please someone else or to make yourself a lovable or adequate person. You will not always please others when you serve them. You can never control the outcome of your activities. Nevertheless, even if others dislike what you did, you will have poured loving energy into your actions.

For many activities the public acknowledgment is shaped like a pyramid: a few people at the very top are widely acclaimed and rewarded, but most of the people work at a lower level and are less known and less rewarded. For every Olympic gymnast idolized on

TV, there are hundreds of thousands of girls in leotards sweating through practices and falling off balance beams. Delight in whatever level you reach in the pyramid of public acknowledgment. You cannot have the tip of the pyramid without all the rest. There is no Nobel Prize winner without thousands of people thinking, learning, teaching, and writing with no dream of any prize. We celebrate the people at the top not for themselves, but as specific examples of the whole pyramid. The moment you forget this, you cheapen the value of your own work and that of everyone else in the pyramid.

From his cage, our half-ounce pet zebra finch, Seedric, sings from sunup to bedtime, sharing his energy with the world. It makes no difference to him if anyone is listening. Out of excess, out of joy, he offers himself in song. Are you willing to offer yourself, out of excess and out of joy—regardless of how anyone out there might judge you, regardless of whether they accept you?

❦ ———————————————————————————— ❦

Practice 113

ACKNOWLEDGE THE JOY OF SERVING

Whatever the event, you are its origin. It is through you, *through* your *will, that God manifests Himself.*

THE MAGGID OF MEZERITCH

Acknowledge and delight in moments of joy through service. It is easy to take your service for granted. The voices come quickly into your mind to suck the value out of what you do: "After all, I'm a nurse, I'm paid to make people feel better." "But mothers are supposed to cook dinner for the family." "What I did is just a drop in the bucket compared to what needs to be done (or compared to what someone else does)."

You will never silence those voices, but that does not mean you have to empower them. Every day, spend a minute reflecting about your moments of service. Do not make comparisons on a path of loving—treasure *all* loving. Silently thank the person or object for being in your life to serve, to let you pour your loving energy into him or it.

Practice 114

LOVE YOUR TOOLS

Where the spirit does not work with the hand there is no art.
LEONARDO DA VINCI

Build a loving relationship with the tools of your activity. Attend with care to your books, instruments, cooking utensils, computer, shoes, bicycle, car, and body. Introduce yourself to them, touch them with care, and make a pact with them to cooperate together to express love.

Practice 115

PAUSE IN A TASK TO CLARIFY
YOUR PURPOSE

Whenever, in the course of the daily hunt, the red hunter comes upon a scene that is strikingly beautiful or sublime—a black thundercloud with the rainbow's glowing arch above the mountain; a white waterfall in the heart of a green gorge; a vast prairie tinged with the blood-red of sunset—he pauses for an instant in the attitude of worship.

OHIYESA

Pause in the middle of a task or a trip. Your experience of an activity is usually diminished if you keep its goal in mind while you do it. Notice how your experience of driving changes when you change focus from *driving to work* to *driving with joy*. In order to break out of an efficient, goal-directed, bottom-line mentality, interrupt whatever you are doing. Stop in the middle, for no purpose at all except to see where you are, appreciate what you are doing and who you are doing it with, delight in the sights and smells, and prove that your real purpose is not to get the task finished. Then recommit to your loving purpose, and go on.

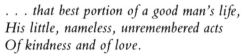

. . . that best portion of a good man's life,
His little, nameless, unremembered acts
Of kindness and of love.

WILLIAM WORDSWORTH

13 ❦ SELF-LOVE—THE JOY OF LIVING

Truly, everything is not lovable that you may love everything; but everything is lovable that you may love the self.

UPANISHADS

The purpose of this chapter is for you to make peace with your self, so that eventually you will relax, pay less attention to that self, and use your life to love all things and delight in being alive.

Your Self-Image

One's self-image *is his own conception of "the sort of person I am." We do not question its validity, but proceed to act upon it just as if it were true. People so act, feel, and behave—even acquire abilities—in such a way as to be consistent with this self-image. In short, you will act like the sort of person you conceive yourself to be.*

MAXWELL MALTZ

In starting to know yourself, the natural first question is, What is a *self*? Since you have been one all your life, you can confront this question based on lifelong experience.

Practice 116

WHO ARE YOU?

The enquiry "Who am I?" is the only method of putting an end to all misery and ushering in supreme Beatitude.

SRI RAMANA MAHARSHI

Head a page in your journal with the question, Who Am I? List the many answers that come to mind. List answers that other people have given you and ones that your internal voices sometimes give. Some of these may contradict others. Head another page, Who Am I Not? Again list as many answers as come to mind. You may find some of the same answers on both lists, since depending on how you look at it, the same response may answer both questions.

Head another page I am _____. Notice how your answers change depending on how you are feeling, on whether the last person you saw smiled or scowled, or on the progress you are making in reaching your current goal.

Countless people have used this as a primary practice in their lifelong spiritual path. One benefit of wrestling with these questions is the realization that who you say you are comes from identifying your self with some feature or pattern from the past or from some frustration or success of the moment. Such identification trivializes what it is to be a human. You are bigger than that.

Practice 117

ON WHAT EVENTS DO YOU BASE YOUR SELF-IMAGE?

He who knows others is wise; he who knows himself is enlightened.
LAO TZU

If you have looked at yourself you will see that you are a bundle of memories . . . of the past or of what you may be in the future, projected from the past.

J. KRISHNAMURTI

Your self-image is a mental model of who and what you are that you use to approach and interpret events. It is based on memories of your past that you selectively recall and on habitual interpretations and generalizations. When you say or think, "I am _____," you attach an all-important notion you call your self to one of your roles or props or memories and to the way you interpret that role or memory. You probably are not even aware of having a self-*image*; it seems to be a true description of who you are. But it is an odd "true description" that changes with every smile or frown, with every success or failure.

You sustain the *I* in your self-image by continuously identifying—that is, making your self identical to something else, treating the two as if they were the same. You see shyness and attach your all-important internal model of *I* to the concept *shy*—thus follows "I am shy."

In this practice, pick one of your answers to the previous practice and head a page with that answer; for example, "I am shy." Then list down one side of the page specific times you can remember when you experienced or behaved in a way you would call shy. Down the other side of the page, list specific times when you experienced or behaved in the opposite way, the way a confident or secure person would.

Do not accept a voice that says you have never done anything confidently. You run risks and engage in the world confidently every day—you just dismiss those times as less important than the times you behave shyly. If you cannot recall a lot of confident events, you are looking for ones that are too big. Settle for smaller ones. Narrow the time span in which you look, to the past week, or just to today.

See how arbitrary is your generalization, "I am shy." If you are shy, you are also confident. You empower the "I am shy" voice because you selectively remember those times when you felt uncomfortable around unfamiliar people. "I am shy" is a self-confirming metaphor through which you see yourself. Now, when you approach people, you chant to yourself, "I am shy, I am shy. This is awful because I am shy." It is no wonder you are uncomfortable, and so your shyness snowballs.

To see what your "I am _____" statements really mean, replace *am* with *as*. "I am shy" means "I as shy,

I see myself *as* shy." You never see your self except through these metaphors. *Is* turns a warm, fluid, verb-like world into a cold space filled with solid nouns. *Is* makes life secure; it allows for prediction and control. But it also demands that you resign yourself to *reality*. *Is* takes the freedom, the possibility, the life out of your life. Whatever your self-image, the more you focus your life around it, the less you can live life afresh, responding now to what is before you.

Practice 118

I AM NOT THAT

He who defines himself can't know who he really is.

LAO TZU

In this ancient practice you begin to shake the solidity out of your self-image. You cultivate a voice that says, "I am not that," in the face of the habitual voice that says you are. Whenever you find your attention drawn to your self-image and how important it is, that is a good time for this practice. It takes the hypnotic power out of "I am" statements, and at least turns them into relatively innocuous "I as" metaphors.

Take each response to the questions "Who am I?" and "I am _____" from Practice 116 and deny the identification your response implies. To answers like "I am shy," deny it and hold up as evidence the many times each day when you act and experience with confidence. To answers like "I am a parent," of course you do not deny the fact that parenting is one of your roles. What you deny is that this role thoroughly defines you, that your role somehow expresses your essence, who *you* are. You are a person playing the role of parent, just as you play many other roles throughout your lifetime. People so commonly identify with their body, their thoughts, and their mechanical behavior that we include separate practices for each.

Practice 119

I AM NOT MY BODY

The purpose is to identify not with the body which is falling away, but with the consciousness of which it is a vehicle.

JOSEPH CAMPBELL

Clearly, you have a physical body that you can experience and control, at least to some extent. But the more you identify your *self* with your body, the more you have to protect that body, worry about its safety, appearance, and health, and divert your attention from whatever is at hand to be done and to be loved. Your body changes dramatically throughout the many years of your life, yet you do not change accordingly. If your legs were amputated, if you lost your sight or hearing, that would change your body and your activities, but not necessarily lessen *you*. *You* are not your body; instead, you *have* a body.

Look into a mirror for perhaps ten minutes and simply *be with* the image of your body, as you experienced being with another person in Practice 54. Notice the internal voices that feel compelled to evaluate the image before you. How important do their judgments seem? Which voice do you habitually empower—the critical one or the reassuring one? Is that body you are looking at *you?* If it is, who just decided to say yes? Who is doing the looking?

Are you willing to give up criticizing this body for how it looks or how it functions? Let other people do that if they want. How grateful can you feel toward it for the countless services it performs for you each day? No matter how infirm or ill your body is, billions of complex processes within it are happening right on schedule every moment or you would not be here. Express your thanks to it. Say "I love you" to your body, and mean it.

Practice 120

I AM NOT MY INTERNAL VOICES

Each thought you have is merely a trial balloon, a draft from your speechwriter sent to you so that you can decide whether you agree or disagree.

BILL HARVEY

You know how strongly your internal voices affect your experiences. It is clear that those voices cannot be *you*, because you can choose which voices to disregard and which ones to take seriously. Disciplined thinking is a great tool for loving, but it is not easy to discipline internal voices. In Practice 19 you listened to them prattling on, planning, analyzing, criticizing, sabotaging your goals, and trashing your purposes. Never satisfied, often repeating old lines from past dramas, these voices seduce you into identifying with them—"Certainly, what else could that voice be, except the true voice of me?"

Take a minute to recall some of the features you like about your image of your self, and tell yourself in your mind how great those features are. Then remember some of the features you dislike about that image and tell yourself how bad those are. To help your memory, look back to your notes in Practice 117 in which you listed the events on which you have based your self-image. Praise you"self" and then criticize your "self," flipping back and forth at will. "I am shy, I am confident." "I am dumb, I am smart." Repeat this practice over and over—say yes to your "self," then no. *You* are not these voices. Instead, *you* are what is listening to them.

This practice shows you how arbitrary the judgment of your self-image is. Your self is not a noun, an object to evaluate or appreciate. You are human, and humans sometimes feel shy and sometimes confident. All humans change with time and can choose the direction they will change.

In self-love there is no object being loved, and no object doing the loving; there is the experience of loving. That is what self-love means. All loving is self-love. The experience of a *yes* directed toward a beloved affirms at the same time the life in which it occurs.

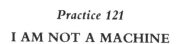

Practice 121

I AM NOT A MACHINE

What is especially interesting about explanations is that they do not explain; and what is especially dangerous about them is that if they are taken seriously enough and far enough, they simply explain things away.

ALAN WATTS

A machine is an object we can explain. It works according to rules and purposes built into it from the outside. Since it has no awareness, it has no choice in its behavior.

Your body, of course, employs physical, chemical, and computational machinery, and your life is constrained by factors like your inheritance, society, nutrition, and past experiences. If you assert that you are *determined* by those constraints, that you are a machine rather than free, you can live in keeping with that belief and your experience will confirm the belief. You will seem to be nothing but a reaction to your structure and to what happens to you. However, if you assert that, constrained as you are by many factors, you are free to make choices, you can live in keeping with that belief. Then your experience will confirm your freedom. It is no wonder that the question of whether people are free or determined has been so hard to settle—whichever view people pick, they can verify it in their lives.

Strengthen your will by exercising it. Pick a frequent activity and head a journal page, Why Do/Did I Do X? List all your considerations about the activity—such as, "The dirty dishes pile up in the sink and there are no clean ones to eat off of." Those are the reasons that are served up by the voice in your mind whose job seems to be to keep explaining life.

In this practice, you put another voice alongside the first. You do not change the considerations—of course the dishes pile up. But you could eat on paper plates. The real reason you are washing the dishes is that *you said you would. You chose to do this.* After considering going out for dinner and leaving the dishes, you chose to wash them.

Make your choices consciously instead of choosing because of the obvious practical considerations. When the phone rings, do not get up to answer it just because it is ringing. You could let it ring. If you answer it, answer it *because you choose to.* At noon, do not eat your lunch because it is time, or because you are hungry; eat it because you choose to. Given the world and yourself as you understand them right now, you have chosen to do this above all else.

This way you replace the machinelike internal conversation of a person run by circumstances with that of a person who is free. Freedom means being able to choose actions and thoughts for yourself, obviously in light of your understanding of yourself and the world. It takes freedom to forge a path of loving in the modern world. You are as free as you learn to be.

Practice 122

I AM THAT

Do I contradict myself?
Very well then I contradict myself,
(I am large, I contain multitudes.)
WALT WHITMAN

In this ancient practice you cultivate a voice that says, "I am that," in the face of habitual voices that distance you from whatever is at hand. It is a vehicle for loving more and for cultivating oneness with the world.

You use "I am that" or "I am part of this" as a mantra, as a practice of compassion and oneness with whatever is at hand. You see a man sifting through the trash can for food, and say, "I am that." Do not just say it, feel it—cold and hungry, looking for something edible among the refuse. You watch the kingfisher, cocky and brash on the power line outside your house, and say, "I am that." Feel the incredible freedom and energy and joy of shouting that raucous call to the world. In this practice you identify your self with anything and everything, not out of habit or feeling that you have no choice, but because you choose to.

Making Peace with Your Past

Into the looking-glass cavern the dog goes running.
Seeing his own reflection, he dies barking.

KABIR

The trouble with your image of your self is the amount of significance you attribute to it, and to your image of other people's images of you. After all, when you were little, your survival seemed hooked to what other people thought of you. They had to feed and protect and love you in order for you to live. Now that you are grown, your survival no longer depends on how they treat you, yet your habits are formed; you have attached the survival of your self to judgments of your self-image.

When judgments of your self seem to control your survival, what happens is important, not for its own sake but for its effect on how you are judged. This turns events into drama and drama into melodrama—"How am I doing?" "What does she think of me?" "Did I do all right?" "I'm not good enough." You live in a conversation in your mind about whether your image of your self measures up to a set of vague standards or expectations. Since you are likely to view yourself as not measuring up, you live in a fog of negativity.

Your relationship with your self is really your relationship with your past. It is the particular memories of what you have done and experienced that you recall and how you interpret or feel about those memories. You make peace with your own past in the same way you make peace with any warring relationship: You reinterpret and go beyond the selective memories of mistakes and hurt that distract your attention from living and loving now.

Practice 123

APPRECIATE YOUR PAST

Knowest thou not the beauty of thine own face? Quit this temper that leads thee to war with thyself!

THE MASNAVI I MA'NAVI

This is a practice in self-acknowledgment, self-appreciation. Start with your journal and think through your entire life to find important events, activities, experiences, and projects you have been responsible for. Look for the way your life has affected others, for memorable feelings you have had, the goals you have achieved. Heading pages in your journal with these phrases will give you the momentum to start: I have been responsible for. . . I have been a caretaker of . . . I have been a cause of . . . I have experienced . . . Here are the areas in which to look for important events.

1. *People.* This might include your family (parents, siblings, spouse, children), colleagues and peers, friends, romantic partners, employers, employees, and others.
2. *The quality of your own life.* Your internal life, the joy, satisfaction, love, and peace you have experienced, as well as the way you bore loss, pain, disappointment, and frustration.

3. *Your body*. How you have used and maintained it, lived with it in good times and bad.
4. *Resources*. How you have used money, tools, opportunities, natural resources, and the support, love, and cooperation of others.
5. *Your accomplishments*. What you have built or achieved and what you have not achieved, the goals you have reached and not reached, the work you have done.
6. *Ideas and skills*. The learning, organizing, creating, doing, growing, sharing, working, and performing involved in all you have done.
7. *Values*. How you moved yourself, others, society, and the world toward a better life.
8. *The world*. Your impact on the people you have touched, objects you have worked with, animals, plants, the earth.
9. *Spiritual growth*. Use your own meaning for this area.

Do not let the fact that you could spend the rest of your life doing this assessment keep you from doing it at all. If you have trouble coming up with items, you are looking for something too important. To break through that barrier, do the practice for events of the past hour and determine to come up with at least twenty items. If you are swamped with items, just choose a few hundred that seem important today.

Just as people offer you a gift when they let you serve them, you give to others by letting them do the same for you. So remember to acknowledge yourself for letting other people love you, serve you, teach you, help you, share with you, work with you, know that you use them as a role model, or contribute to your growth. You give to your parents or teachers when you let them love or teach you.

If items come to mind that pull you with a heartfelt *no*, add them to Practice 126 below.

Now acknowledge yourself for having caused each item on your list. Value and appreciate every one—

you did that, you caused that. You have done well, have loved, have learned, have helped others. Ripples from your life, as they move out into the world, are good ripples. Validate them. You have poured much loving energy into the world, and you have experienced much love.

Get together with a friend or family member and share your list of items as a series of triumphs. Allow a block of at least thirty minutes, perhaps much more, and, item after item, acknowledge your past to this person. Their job is simply to understand what you are saying and get a sense of the difference your life has made. Theirs is an exercise in loving while listening, so they interrupt you only by some nodding of the head and a few appreciative comments.

How hard is it for you to accept the growth and accomplishment in your life? Do you automatically turn your power over to an invalidating voice and mechanically, out of habit, hedge on everything positive and cling to the negative about yourself? "Yes, but lots of people did it even better than I." "Yes, but we broke up two months later." "Yes, but that wasn't the best I was capable of doing." Will you give up this incessant "yes, but"? Will you accept and value your past—in words, tone of voice, posture, and facial expression? Will you really put your heart into meaning it?

This practice breaks the "yes, but" habit. It is loving your memories of your past—selectively recalling and interpreting them with a heartfelt yes. Surely that is cultivating one form of self-love.

Practice 124

MAKE PEACE WITH YOUR RELATIONSHIP WITH YOUR SELF

A man prayed to the Master to pardon his sins. He was told that it would be enough if he took care to see that his mind did not trouble him.

SRI RAMANA MAHARSHI

In this practice you use the methods of Chapter 9 to make peace with the memories, habits, and limitations that draw you into a heartfelt no directed at yourself. At the top of a journal page write the question, What keeps me from loving myself? Put down the answers that come to mind, however contradictory and illogical they may be. In order to generate more answers, head a page, I do not love my self because _____. List as many reasons as you can.

With each one of these, systematically go through the practices of Chapter 9 for keeping your relationships at peace. You may need to cycle through those practices many times in order to make peace with some memories, but the work will free you to love more deeply and more often. Surely it is worth the effort to make peace with memories of your own past.

Practice 125

VIEW YOUR LIFE FROM BEGINNING TO END

Think that you are not yet begotten, that you are in the womb, that you are young, that you are old, that you have died, that you are in the world beyond the grave; grasp in your thoughts all this at once, all times and places, all substances and qualities and magnitudes together; then you can apprehend God.

HERMES

This is sometimes called the Hermetic Practice, since Hermes (the priestly wisdom of ancient Egypt) taught it 2,200 years ago as a way to change oneself into "eternal substance." See yourself as standing at a huge canvas, paintbrush in hand. Depending on the colors available and the canvas at the moment, you paint your life, the colors going from your brush to the canvas, where lies the past. You can do nothing about the paint once it falls. You, like all the other painters, at your own part of this huge canvas, have laid it down, and there it will stay forever as part of the history of the universe.

All you can do about the past is to choose what to look at, how to look at it, how to interpret it, what story you tell about it, and what you will learn from it.

The paint always passes on its way from a possible future into a particular past, and it is your choices that put it onto the canvas, turning possibility into reality. Objects, thoughts, people, loves, pains, opportunities —you keep adding these brushstrokes one by one. By your choices you create both physical events and your internal experience of those events. You realize a moment of joy as surely as you realize a well-cooked dinner. All goes on the canvas.

So long as you live, you stand at your canvas, building your life, brushstroke by brushstroke, choosing, watching, and loving. There are no mistakes on the canvas, nothing that needs to be fixed. You can keep taking responsibility for the picture, for choosing what you choose out of what is available to you. The world is a dramatic record to which you contribute as director, actor, and audience. And the audience is part of the show. You do not direct all of it. Some of the plot lines are contributed by others, and some were laid down before you got on stage. You do not act all the roles. You do not even see all of it. Your share is just a part of it, but an indispensable part!

Be sure to notice the experiences in your life-painting. All your loving is on the canvas. When you have created meaning out of confusion or hopelessness, you have put that meaning onto the painting. When you transform pain or loss into triumph, you have, once and for all, painted that triumph into the record.

Have compassion for yourself, a fallible human being whose life lies there before you. It started as an infant with your particular parents in your particular culture. It will run until you have brought your last possibility from the future through the reality of the moment into the security of the past. Say yes to what you have done, to when you have loved, and to when you have disappointed yourself and others. All of it has been your lot as a human being.

You still stand at the canvas, brush in hand. Now you can paint your life knowingly, proudly, rejoicing in everything. You do not know what significance your life has in the universe, but you can trust that by loving you are contributing to that significance.

> *The fingers and strings—*
> *They do not comprehend the ultimate reality of the music.*
> RABINDRANATH TAGORE

Self-Love

Every man is his own masterpiece.

HENRY DAVID THOREAU

In order to cultivate self-love, you have to decide what self-love is. Appreciating and making peace with your own past is surely one form of self-love. If you determine what is worthy of love by judging merit, you put yourself into a world in which judging is all-important. The voice of fear (sometimes labeled *ego*) then says you must have special merit in order to say yes to yourself.

In order to create a separate self, you must draw boundaries between you and others. One way to create boundaries is by saying no, while saying yes is the way to oneness. No is the route of ego—"I don't like that, I won't have that." Yes is humbling—"I'm willing to have even that." On a loving path you dissolve the voice of ego by constantly saying yes, regardless of circumstances.

Conceit means comparing yourself to others. Argue against the voice that says self-love is the recognition that you have especially good qualities. You have human qualities, which could be judged good and could be judged bad.

Whatever your limitations and whatever your past, your human qualities alone are good enough for self-love.

It is not your lot as a human being to know what the nounlike, objectlike qualities of your self are, but you may be able to conclude what your self *does* as you go through life. Imagine yourself standing before the canvas containing the record of the past (see Practice 125), painting it as you live. From moment to moment, what do you do? You *choose*—what to paint, how to approach the painting, and how to interpret it. And you *experience*—the act of painting and of seeing the canvas before you. Perhaps that is all you do—experience and choose.

Practice 126

DELIGHT IN ALL ASPECTS OF BEING ALIVE

It is not the body that you love, it is Life—perceiving, feeling, thinking, doing, loving, striving, creating. It is that Life you love, which is you, which is all.

SRI NISARGADATTA MAHARAJ

In this practice you break through the old inhibitions against reveling in all aspects of being alive—your body, your past, your abilities, your awareness, your freedom. This is the time to be exuberant. Look at yourself in the mirror, call yourself by name, and say "(Name), I love you." Recall an event from your past and rejoice that it is there, in the grand painting, where it will stay forever. Experience what you see with fresh eyes, what you hear with fresh ears, what you taste with a fresh tongue, and rejoice in it all. Say, "Life is wonderful," and view it through that wonder. Send yourself love. Affirm yourself: "I am loving." "I'm so glad to be alive." See yourself with joy and compassion, living as best you can on your path of loving, sometimes confused, sometimes faltering, but always human. Hug that person on that path. Send yourself a blessing.

Practice 127

TEACH ONLY LOVE

Teach only love, for that is what you are.

A COURSE IN MIRACLES

For ten minutes each day see yourself as truly a God-like being with the delicious task of spreading Light wherever you are. See yourself as unabashedly giving love and delight, as smiling, as believing in peace and in joy and in the absence of pain. Try it. You will find that it is the most contagious thing you have ever caught.

EMMANUEL (PAT RODEGAST)

Try the practice described above by Emmanuel. Love as if you were a master teacher, teaching loving to others—because you *are* teaching it to others, to all the others who come in contact with you. Whenever you are uncertain what you do, ask yourself what a master teacher of loving would do in this situation.

Sometimes I go about
In pity for myself
And all the while
A great wind is bearing me across the sky.

OJIBWA POEM

14 ❦ GOD AS A PATH TO LOVING AND LOVING AS A PATH TO GOD

And an old priest said, Speak to us of Religion. And he said: Have I spoken this day of aught else?

KAHLIL GIBRAN

T he purpose of this chapter is for you to see how you might, if you choose, use your view of God to deepen the love and meaning with which you experience life, and in turn to use the love and meaning in your life to deepen your view of God.

Spiritual Skills and Religious Beliefs

> *Quite apart from our religion*
> *There are plum blossoms,*
> *There are cherry blossoms.*
>
> NANPOKU

What matters today is not the difference between those who believe and those who do not believe, but the difference between those who care and those who don't.

ABBÉ PIRE

When you determine to walk a path of loving, you accept a spiritual challenge from life. While such a path also challenges your intellect, your body, and all your skills, its essence is a challenge to your spirit—to deepen your experience with meaning and love, regardless of circumstances, and to pour loving energy into the world.

The different religious traditions offer countless stories and memories that people can use to meet their spiritual challenge and enrich their experience of events. In centuries past, people never got to choose their religions—they were handed one at birth as the only true religious structure, monolithic within their culture. They had to face their spiritual challenge within that one structure.

Today you confront your spiritual challenge with unheard-of religious freedom. Different religions are as near as your phone, your car, or your bookstore. You are free to dismiss as mere superstition the traditions that dominated the lives of hundreds of generations of people. You are also free to draw on traditions known in the past to only a few.

Religious traditions, honed to survive in a monoculture, are slow to adapt to the polyculture. From within them, change is heresy. The most common belief about reality is that there is only one. People crave agreement and insist that others believe just what they do. The more folks who believe alike, the easier it is for them to keep believing.

When a group of people have a set of religious beliefs that seems to work for them, they credit the working to the beliefs, not to their own skill at using the beliefs. They are sure that everyone would benefit from those beliefs. Since there is only one reality, theirs must be the only possible beliefs that could work.

Thus, religious traditions pay great attention to *what* people believe. Unfortunately, they tend to neglect the spiritual skills of *how* to use those beliefs to meet spiritual challenges.

Practice 128

WHAT DOES *GOD* MEAN TO YOU?

Our idea of God tells us more about ourselves than about Him.

THOMAS MERTON

The search for God is like riding around on an ox hunting for the ox.

BUDDHIST SAYING

In this practice you clarify the meanings you bring to any discussion involving God. Head a journal page, What Does *God* Mean to Me? List as many meanings as come to mind. That includes not only your particular beliefs about God but also how God relates to your life. Head another page with, What Does *Sacred* Mean to Me?

 ————————————————————

The Nature of Beliefs

It's not easy to experience the unfamiliar, the unnamed. We say, "If I hadn't seen it with my own eyes, I wouldn't have believed it." But the phrase really should be, "If I hadn't believed it with all my heart, I wouldn't have seen it."

EDMUND CARPENTER

Consider what it means to believe in something—say, your front door. You carry an elaborate model in your head of the world outside you. You have had some experiences of what people call your door, so you have built it into the model you ground your life on. You believe in that door; indeed, you know where it is and how to use it. You take its existence for granted, never doubt it, and live *as if* it exists. Whenever you want to enter or leave your house, you just go to your door and it works.

These days, if you think there is only one kind of believing—the same kind you use for your door—then belief in God seems impossible. Whereas you do not seem to have much choice about the door, you have unlimited choice about God. In this polyculture, you will not find just one way of thinking about God that seems true while all the others seem false. Everyone who talks about God has something different in mind.

You may decide either to give up on God altogether or to settle for *having faith* in God instead. Faith seems to mean that you have less direct experience of God, less evidence for believing, less proof, and more hope. So you close your eyes to your lack of evidence and jump.

But there is no point in jumping unless the jump *works* to meet your spiritual challenge—deepening your experience and breathing meaning, life, and love into your existence. Just as believing in a door will not help you get out of the house if you do not know how to turn the latch, no amount of belief by itself will help you on your loving path. You know people who hold all kinds of religious beliefs and others who scorn such beliefs as delusions, with no apparent effect on their loving. It takes spiritual skills to love, not religious beliefs.

Living As If

When a belief becomes more than an instrument, you are lost. You remain lost until you learn what "belief" is really for.

IDRIES SHAH

The secret of a warrior is that he believes without believing. . . . To just believe would exonerate him from examining his situation. A warrior, whenever he has to involve himself with believing, does it as a choice.

DON JUAN (CARLOS CASTANEDA)

And now here is my secret, a very simple secret; it is only with the heart that one can see rightly; what is essential is invisible to the eye.

ANTOINE DE SAINT–EXUPERY

Handling belief the way Don Juan suggests means willfully *living as if* something is true for the purpose of experiencing the world through its truth, thereby bolstering your belief and loving more deeply. Because you are not used to choosing these "as ifs" for yourself, they may feel contrary to fact. When you do not pour yourself into them, they *are* contrary to fact, but they become fact when you do. They are truths waiting to be created by someone with the will to create them.

You could live as if you are already approved of, forgiven, regardless of whatever you may have done—and as if other people, too, are forgiven, whether or not you approve of their behavior. You could live as if you trust the universe that created you to know what it is up to, even when you do not like what is happening.

You need not believe literally in your loving "as ifs." The fact that you must invest yourself in holding them as true is what makes them useful spiritually. This question of literal truth has always plagued people wrestling with religious belief, faith, and doubt. Your front door is going to be the way in and out of your house regardless of how you approach it. But in order to use the notion that God is in this rose to enhance your love of the rose, you have to do more than say, "Oh, yes, that is God." You use the words, "This is God," to evoke your surrender to the rose in awe and oneness. It is surrender that makes the rose divine, not something it had before you came along.

Thus, believing or not believing in God is not the issue. When godliness is inside you, you project it outward and you see God. Of course, that has been true with people through all time, and true of the countless images of God that they held. That is why there have been so many gods in the history of humanity. Different images lead to different realities, behavior, and experience, and nonloving images of God lead to nonloving lives. If you are following a loving path, your ultimate concern is loving. Then your God is love.

Practice 129

WHAT BELIEFS WOULD EMPOWER YOU TO LOVE?

Belief consists in accepting the affirmations of the soul; unbelief in denying them.

RALPH WALDO EMERSON

Explore in your journal the question, What beliefs would empower me to love more deeply, if only I held them? What beliefs would help to bring an end to your deepest fears? What beliefs would comfort your grief ? What beliefs would permit you to trust the universe or God, to give you confidence that life and the world were proceeding as they should? What beliefs would help you look forward to the future, not only your own but the future of humanity and the world? What beliefs would turn your work into an outpouring of loving energy into the world? What beliefs would deepen your love for your family, friends, and others? In Emerson's words, what are the "affirmations of the soul" that your mind will not allow you to believe?

In our culture it is hard to hold these beliefs: "If only I could believe that my work made a real difference to anyone." "If only I believed that God had a plan for the universe and that life, including my own life, was not a meaningless accident." Such beliefs sound so naive—who could hold them as true?

You could hold them as true—not as reactive beliefs as you have with your front door, where you have no choice but to believe, but as intentional beliefs, where you deliberately pick one of them and *live as if* it is true.

Practice 130

PRACTICE "LIVING AS IF"

Faith is not blind. It is the willingness to try.

SRI NISARGADATTA MAHARAJ

This is the first of several practices in which you approach a situation while deliberately holding a belief about it that enhances your experience. Use your creativity to come up with a belief that deepens your heartwarming experience. Then hold that belief as intensely as you can while in that situation.

Watch the stream sparkling in the sunlight as if the sun is dancing for joy in the water. Listen to the cries of the hungry, the abused, the abandoned as if they are the cries of your own children. Hear the cicada singing you to sleep as if the universe is playing a violin for your personal delight. See all the creatures on earth as if they are your brothers and sisters. See your "enemies" and your country's "enemies" as if they are people like you—lonely, scared, and dangerous only because they are scared. Live as if humanity is created with enough sense to make it through the challenges of the future in peace and fulfillment.

Pick one of the beliefs from the list you made in Practice 129 and work to live as if it were true. When you go to work, know which people directly benefit from your work, even if they never acknowledge you, and vividly imagine your efforts and care rippling through your community. When you are inclined to get cynical, know that God's plan for the universe is being realized and that all life, your own included, is involved in mutual loving, sharing, and growth. How intensely can you pour yourself into these practices? What is the effect on your experience?

Practice 131

SEE A MIRACLE

Anyone who doesn't believe in miracles is not a realist.

DAVID BEN-GURION

As to me I know of nothing else but miracles.

WALT WHITMAN

In this practice you deliberately experience whatever is around you and your own awareness of it as a miracle. A miracle is something extraordinary, something whose existence in your life you do not understand. A miracle is something whose presence you marvel at, something you cannot explain away, whose cause is not obvious or trivial.

If you are willing to approach the world and its so-called explanations with awe, the explanations simply compound one mystery with another. Explanations explain away a mystery only if you give them that power. The question is, Who is boss? You do not need to cling to what you have been taught by a culture that is still learning how to live richly while dominated by scientific models.

Assume the attitude of awe or wonder, and approach something with that attitude. It could be your toothbrush, the water you use to brush your teeth, or your daily newspaper. Reflect on what caused it to be in your life. View with amazement the many events that brought it to you. The universe and all consciousness in it are caused out of mystery, and all chains of cause and effect lead back to mystery. Cultivate a state of mind in which you use the chain of causes, "This was caused by that, which was caused by something else . . ." in order to increase your wonder and delight.

Practice seeing the miraculous in as simple an object as a pebble, and in as complex a creature as a person. Lie on your back and look at the heavens on a clear night, and as you do, know that countless billions of people have done the same before you. Screen your life for miracles and revel in the experience of finding them.

God as Your Ultimate Concern

God is that which concerns us ultimately.
PAUL TILLICH

God is an abstraction the way *humanity* is. With Tillich's notion of God, it is the object of your ultimate concern. Not just your concern or your real concern, but your *ultimate concern*. With that notion, you can love God in a concrete incarnation—in the warmth of this person or of that sunshine.

To do this, take the stand that you *will find the ultimate in the immediate;* that is, you *will* find God in this object, animal, or person before you. Your recognition of the sacred in the ordinary does not follow from the sacredness or ordinariness of what you experience. Ordinary and sacred are two ways of looking at the same thing. You are not loving this person or sunshine just because it is special. On a path of loving, the specialness of each individual becomes your vehicle to love the whole. It is not this form before you, but God you are loving. The forms are human or tree or cloud, and only the forms are present to you.

> *Those eyes—yes, those—are God's;*
> *The eyes you gaze into and the eyes you see with.*
> *This hand—yes, this—is God's;*
> *The hand you touch and the hand you touch with.*

❦ ———————————————————————————— ❦

Practice 132

FIND GOD IN SOMETHING NEARBY

I hear and behold God in every object, yet I understand God not in the least.

WALT WHITMAN

The ideal of man is to see God in everything. But if you cannot see Him in everything, see Him in one thing, in that thing which you like best, and then see Him in another. So on you can go.

VIVEKANANDA

Approach something nearby as if it is God, with the awe, the wonder, the ultimate meaning and concern that you associate with God. How deep a concern can you bring to it? How rich a meaning can you bestow upon it? This object before you partakes of the *ultimate,* and it is here for you to appreciate, to delight in. Do justice to it.

Living as if is not some leap of belief, but a freely chosen stance you take toward life. Here you practice living as if the object is sacred, is God. You always *live as if.* You can't help but approach life as if it is something, even if it is just one more dull event that fills up your day. But you are free to choose. You could live as if your life depends on loving. You could live as if God put you here for the purpose of loving and learning.

Express your ultimate concern for whatever is before you. Hug your daughter as if she is all the humanity that will follow after you, caress your lover as if his is the body of God, pet your dog as if it is all of life in the universe, and scrub the floor as if it is a sacred offering to your family and the world. Throw yourself into loving approaches even if they seem silly, in order to free yourself from old habits of "I can't" and "It's ridiculous." Throw yourself into your *as if.* Make it more real than what you normally call the real world. Live *as if* with all your heart, sometimes for short periods and sometimes for long periods. Strengthen this skill as you go through life.

 ————————————————————————

Practice 133

TURN THIS ACTION INTO A SACRAMENT

The world is imprisoned in its own activity, except when actions are performed as worship of God. Therefore perform every action sacramentally.

BHAGAVAD GITA

Sacraments are actions you turn into sacred mysteries through willful dedication to spiritual meanings. The difference between secular and sacramental action is how deeply you intend or will a spiritual expression, such as celebration, joy, sensitivity, surrender, and wonder.

Make this action a sacrament. Let your actions enhance the sacred mystery of your life through willful dedication or consecration. Express meaning through your actions and they will in turn call forth or evoke meaning. When you pull a weed, bless the whole earth that is feeding your children and countless subsequent generations. Turn your touch into a caress, your speech into poetry and song, your movements into grace and dance, your glance into caring.

Meditate on doing some workaday task as sacrament, in deep love—cooking or walking or talking. Rehearse this behavior: What will you say to yourself as you next take this action? How will you say it? Then when you next do this task, you will not forget what you intended; your rehearsed approach will capture your mind and actions.

 ——————————————————————

God as Love

God is love; and he that dwells in love dwells in God, and God in him.

ST. JOHN

The statement "God is love" is not completely clear. But do not get tangled up in worrying about whether God is your beloved, or God is actually loving through you, or God is the loving experience, or God is the thought of loving or the will to love, or simply that loving is Godlike. If your ultimate concern is loving, then "God is love" means all of these ideas. You can put energy into any one of them to enhance the spiral of love.

In Practice 132 you work with the idea of God as your beloved. Work with these other ideas of God as love to see how much they help you deepen your loving.

Practice 134

LOVE AS GOD

Love is God.
LEO TOLSTOY

The best way to know God is to love many things.
VINCENT VAN GOGH

In this practice you approach a beloved as if it is God who is loving through you. You are a channel for the care, the delight, the heartfelt *yes* of God. As you create *yes* in appreciating this beloved, God creates *yes*. You are loving, not as a little clod of earth, but as the loving spirit of the universe. You are taking literally the statement, "God is love," and you are acting on it.

Practice 135

ACCEPT A HEARTFELT YES FROM GOD

This Great God, like a mother bending over her baby,
Kneeled down in the dust toiling over a lump of clay
Till He shaped it in His own image;
Then into it He blew the breath of life,
And man became a living soul. Amen. Amen.
JAMES WELDON JOHNSON

In Practice 26 you experienced the inputs of your senses as the love of the universe directed toward you. In this practice you go further and live as if the *yes* that everything in the universe is directing toward you is the love of God. Accept that God said yes in order for you to be born; that God says yes to you in providing you with air for each breath, with each meal, with each glass of water; that God says yes to you in every friend, every relative, every birdsong, and every sparkling dewdrop. Accept that you are sustained every moment by a heartfelt yes from God via the universe, and that if that were not the case, you would not be here. Let the love of God in, feel it, accept it. Do not second-guess God. It is OK for God to love you—you deserve it. Who else should know better? "God is love" means that God loves *you,* affirms *you.*

Practice 136

PRAYER—TURN REQUESTS INTO AFFIRMATIONS

For the Great Spirit is everywhere: He hears whatever is in our minds and hearts, and it is not necessary to speak to Him in a loud voice.

BLACK ELK

Prayer and affirmations are deeply linked; the prayer, "Fill my heart with love," may become the affirmation,"My heart is full of love." In a way, finding an affirmation is a response to prayer.
ALBERTO KONIGSBERG (WILLIAM ASHOKA ROSS)

This is the practice suggested by Konigsberg. Make a list in your journal of personal requests that you would make if you had God's ear, of what you would ask for if prayer consisted of asking God for favors or blessings. For each item on your list, visualize that not only do you have God's ear, but visualize life as if you had already received the item. Write out an affirmation, a statement that you already are blessed with it. You can make the affirmation short, as "My heart is full of love," or you can amplify the affirmation into a paragraph or page detailing what life with this blessing is like.

Having written these affirmations, put them where you will see them and read them over often. Record them on audiotape and play them for yourself when you are waking up, driving, working, or going to bed. This practice will change your life from one of emptiness or neediness to one of fullness.

Practice 137

LET YOUR LIFE BE YOUR PRAYER

Prayer is the contemplation of the facts of life from the highest point of view. It is the soliloquy of a beholding and jubilant soul. It is the spirit of God pronouncing his works good.

RALPH WALDO EMERSON

You can understand life in several ways. When you understand it as a question demanding explanation, you get the path of science. When you understand it as a celebration or a mystery demanding deepening, you get the path of loving. You can walk more than one path at the same time. Life is bigger than your understandings.

If the concept of prayer has meaning for you, then let your loving be praying—the heartfelt affirmation of the creature to the creator, your witness to the divine in life and the world.

Let your life be your prayer, crafted specially to express your love. Regardless of whether the concept of prayer has meaning for you, see your loving as the perfect response of a conscious being to life, an intrinsically good part of the snowballing love that will fill this planet.

And what if it were true after all? Tell me, and what if it were true?

REBBE LEVI–YITZHAK

15 ❦ BEING COMMITTED TO LOVING

Something we were withholding made us weak,
Until we found it was ourselves.

ROBERT FROST

T he question is how to use this book to be more than just another book, how to use it to fill your life with enthusiasm, delight, and wonder. Inertia says just go on as before, and keep hoping for something or someone so marvelously attractive to come along that you will react to it with loving.

But the path of loving is not a path of attraction in contrast to repulsion; it is a path of commitment in contrast to forgetfulness. Loving is commitment to thinking, seeing, and acting with a *yes*, despite sometimes unwanted circumstances and lifelong habits to the contrary. These habits, strong as they are, are only habits, and they can be replaced by loving habits if you simply remember.

Commitment

You learn to love by loving. . . . Begin as a mere apprentice, and the very power of love will lead you on to become a master in the art.

ST. FRANCIS OF SALES

Commitment brings peace of mind; not the end of the journey, but the end of wandering; not the end of a road, but the end of searching for one.

LESLIE WEATHERHEAD

To commit to a loving purpose means to assert that you *will* regularly practice loving and you *will* let loving play a larger and larger role in your everyday choices. With that assertion, you hand future choices over for safekeeping to the promise you have made. Then, in the bustle of daily life, you base choices on what you said you would do, rather than on old habits or how you feel at the moment or what other people might approve of. Even when you have forgotten the original motivation behind the commitment, you know that your life works better when you keep your word and stay on purpose, so you do what you said you would.

Commitment gives life a thrust of purpose, so you are not tossed here and there by every fear and desire. Acting out of a commitment changes the meaning of what might otherwise be a gesture or an accident into constructive, life-long behavior.

Practice 138

COMMIT TO A PATH OF LOVING

Whatever you can do, or dream you can, begin it.
Boldness has genius, power and magic in it.

GOETHE

It is better to begin in the evening than not at all.

ENGLISH PROVERB

In this practice you write out your commitment to a path of loving. What vision do you hold of how your life will be on such a path? How and when will you practice loving? How will you include your commitment in your day-to-day choices, actions, and conversations? How will your commitment affect your work, family, friends, body, intellect? How willing are you to keep your commitment to this path?

Share your commitment statement with a friend. Write it out and post it where you will read it every day. Record it on audiotape and play it frequently.

Commitment is your primary tool for changing the habits of a lifetime. Treat it with your deepest respect.

Practice 139

KEEP YOUR WORD

My life was a risk—and I took it!
ROBERT FROST

Commitment means we haven't left ourselves an escape hatch.
CHARLOTTE JOKO BECK

This is the practice of keeping your commitment—practicing loving and letting loving play a role in your choices—throughout each day. It is a continual practice in mindfulness in which your purpose is expressed in your commitment statement. Do not look just to your current feelings to tell you what to do—look to your commitment. Feelings are like clouds, moving across your consciousness on every breeze. Loving is not just a feeling; it is also a voice within you that you empower, and an action that you decide to make.

Note in your journal your progress and what pulls you off purpose, and visualize what you will do tomorrow under the same circumstances to stay on track.

Practice 140

HAVE COMPASSION FOR YOURSELF

Simply view yourself as a pioneer in the long journey of increasing consciousness. We started millions of years ago. No doubt we will not finish tomorrow.

KEN KEYES, JR.

To commit to loving demands that you rise above the fear that you will not keep your word, and the belief that if you do not keep your word you should indulge in self-damning by way of punishment. Self-damning, hurling criticism at yourself because you are a fallible human being, detours you from a path of loving. It stems from the belief that a good person does not make mistakes, so if you make a mistake, in order to remain a good person you should condemn yourself for making it.

Disappointing yourself is just another occasion for compassion, for understanding that as a human being you are certain to keep disappointing yourself in one way or another. The trap lies not in disappointing yourself, but in berating yourself for disappointing yourself. A path of loving has no goal, only a purpose. You are always walking your path. If you find yourself going in a direction you do not like, simply change direction and keep walking. Since progress in growth and loving is rare, treasure it, honor it, celebrate it when it occurs. When you seem to be making no progress, learn what you can and go on. There is no place to get to. Life is not a task, it is a joyful journey.

Practice 141

MEDITATE ON A QUOTATION OR EVENT

Work of sight is done.
Now do heart work
On the pictures within you.
RAINER MARIA RILKE

Pick a quotation from this book, or a story, passage, poem, song, artwork, dance, idea from science, or event from your past, and let it move you to warmth, openness, and trust. Allocate ten or fifteen minutes to reading, speaking, thinking about, looking at, listening to, recalling, feeling this work or memory. Set a timer and keep your mind focused on the work. Become one with it. Write freely about it. Let it evoke as positive an experience as you can. If voices say this is meaningless, the wrong topic, that you want to quit, just notice them and go back to the work. Let the timer tell you when to end. This practice assures that you spend more time with the most positive elements in your culture and less time with the negative.

What Is Human Life?

Be glad of life! Because it gives you the chance to love and work, to play and to look up at the stars.

HENRY VAN DYKE

However you answer the question, What is a human being?, your answer evokes experience that confirms the answer. So be careful when you approach such questions and give only answers that you want confirmed in your life.

A few things about human beings are obviously true: They are consciousness incarnate, they are lovers and learners, they evolved to cooperate and they thrive on cooperation, they are seekers of visions, they are free to choose, and they are creatures of sharing and trust.

Human life is a journey from birth to death in which people love and learn, and from which they take none of their trophies. A person's roles and possessions, such as marriage, job, and community, are not things but possibilities. A marriage, for example, is an opportunity, a possibility, a challenge to see how much loving it can contain. A house, while it is a physical object, presents itself to a person as a possibility to turn it into the warmth and love of a home.

Practice 142

WHAT IS HUMAN LIFE?

Life is a song—sing it.
Life is a game—play it.
Life is a challenge—meet it.

Life is a dream—realize it.
Life is a sacrifice—offer it.
Life is love—enjoy it.

SAI BABA

In this practice, you write your own answers to the question, What is a human life? or you repeatedly complete the sentence, "Human life is a _____." When a negative or cynical answer comes to mind, look at it to see which voice is saying that. Why do some of your voices seem to take pride in sabotaging the positive? What might they be protecting you from? Do they really protect? Are there ways you can feel safe other than empowering such voices?

Reflect on your list and see how positively, how powerfully, you can view humanity. See your own life and those of everyone else from this vantage point. The *yes* you generate toward yourself and others will ripple through the world and multiply many times in the process.

Practice 143

CREATE A POSITIVE VISION OF THE FUTURE

As you walk, you cut open and create that riverbed into which the stream of your descendants shall enter and flow. . . . Let us unite, let us hold each other tightly, let us merge our hearts . . . and so long as the warmth of this earth endures, let us create for earth a brain and a heart, let us give a human meaning to the superhuman struggle.

NIKOS KAZANTZAKIS

Although people are as free as they assert themselves to be, we are also products of our culture. Those who have gone before make the opportunities and limitations that are realized by those who follow. Thus your life inescapably creates a world for those who come after you. And the vision you hold of the future affects not only what you do, but the love with which you do it.

Write out a positive statement of the vision you hold for the world—in perhaps ten years, fifty years, and two hundred years. When negative images come to mind, acknowledge that they have validity, but imagine that humanity will have the wisdom to bypass them. Share your positive images of the world with others. Hold your images before you as you do your life's work, and know that by your life you are contributing to turning Earth into a planet of love.

Practice 144

WRITE LETTERS ACKNOWLEDGING YOUR LIFE

If the only prayer you say in your whole life is "thank you," that would be enough.

MEISTER ECKHART

If you were going to die soon and had only one phone call you could make, who would you call and what would you say? And why are you waiting?

STEPHEN LEVINE

The first part of this practice is to write a letter to the universe, to God, or to all of life, expressing thanks for your life. Times when circumstances make you feel this is impossible are especially suitable times to do it. You can thank the universe even with tears in your eyes. Mention specific people, objects, abilities, and opportunities for which you are especially grateful, and include personal thank-yous. If any of the people you mention are still alive, send them copies of the part about them, if that is appropriate. Read this letter over from time to time and keep it up to date as your life evolves.

The second part of this practice is to write a letter as if it were written shortly after your death by someone who knows and loves you, to someone else who knows and loves you. If you cannot think of such people who are likely to be alive at the time of your death, make some up. In the letter, have the writer reflect back over your life as he knows it firsthand, secondhand, and through intuition. Have him interpret your life with deep compassion, respect, appreciation, and humor—whatever is appropriate to a positive expression of who you were and what you stood for. This is not the time for modesty, this is the time for writing a moving vision of your entire life as seen by someone who loves you completely, someone who understands what it is to be the particular, unique human being that you are, someone who articulates a vision of your life that you can measure up to and can rejoice in completing.

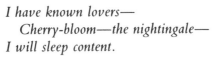

> *I have known lovers—*
> *Cherry-bloom—the nightingale—*
> *I will sleep content.*
>
> ANONYMOUS

About the Author

Frank Andrews grew up in Manhattan, Kansas. Educated as a scientist, he graduated from Kansas State University and received a Ph.D. from Harvard. Since 1967, he has been a professor at the University of California, Santa Cruz. He has studied at several major universities in the United States and Europe, has written several books on chemical physics, and has been awarded many honors for his scientific work and his teaching. He has taught at the University of Wisconsin, Harvard, and Dartmouth.

Since 1975, his primary field of study and teaching has been general problem solving, psychological unblocking, learning how people's values affect their lives, and how to love life regardless of circumstances. In this work he has read over a thousand books, attended and led endless hours of workshops, and counseled innumerable students. Trained as a physical scientist, he searches for ideas and techniques that have power to affect people's lives. His approach is to make order out of confusing intellectual messes. This publication is his first nonscience book—on loving because he is convinced that it is the most important topic there is.

He and his wife and their two daughters live in Santa Cruz.